Education of Culturally and Linguistically Different Exceptional Children

A product of the ERIC Clearinghouse on Handicapped and Gifted Children

The Council for Exceptional Children

371.967
Ed 83

Edited by Philip C. Chinn

LIBRARY
ATLANTIC CHRISTIAN COLLEGE
WILSON N. C.

Library of Congress Cataloging in Publication Data
Main entry under title:

Education of culturally and linguistically different exceptional children.

   "A product of the ERIC Clearinghouse on Handicapped and Gifted Children."
   1. Children of immigrants--Education--United States--Addresses, essays,
lectures. 2. Handicapped children--Education--United States--Addresses,
essays, lectures. 3. Education, Bilingual--United States--Addresses, essays,
lectures. 4. Native language and education--United States--Addresses,
essays, lectures. 5. Cognition in children--United States--Addresses,
essays, lectures. I. Chinn, Philip C., 1937-   . II. ERIC Clearinghouse on
Handicapped and Gifted Children.
LC3731.E39 1984   371.96'7   84-27450
ISBN 0-86586-152-8

A product of the ERIC Clearinghouse on Handicapped and Gifted Children.

Published in 1984 by The Council for Exceptional Children, 1920 Association
Drive, Reston, Virginia 22091-1589.

This publication was prepared with funding from the National
Institute of Education, US Department of Education, under contract
no. 400-81-0031. Contractors undertaking such projects under
government sponsorship are encouraged to express freely their judgment in
professional and technical matters. Prior to publication the manuscript was
submitted to The Council for Exceptional Children for critical review and
determination of professional competence. This publication has met such
standards. Points of view, however, do not necessarily represent the official
view or opinions of either The Council for Exceptional Children, the National
Institute of Education, or the Department of Education.

Printed in the United States of America.

CONTENTS

FEB 21 1986

Ed. 8.04

85- 1750

PREFACE

In the spring of 1979, I was asked for assistance by a local school district in suggesting the appropriate programming for a mentally retarded Chinese student who was unable to speak English. While this was not the type of service my office usually provided, my curiosity prompted me to agree to go to the school and at least assess the situation. What I found was a young Chinese immigrant girl, Ming, who spoke no English and had only limited comprehension in Cantonese. Unable to evaluate her adequately, the school personnel assumed her to be trainable mentally retarded. The bilingual education program in this district wanted no part of her since she was obviously a special education problem. The special education staff could not communicate with her in Cantonese and felt that she should be the responsiblity of bilingual education personnel. Each day Ming would do nothing but sit quietly by herself on the floor of her classroom.

Since 1979, a number of higher education programs have emerged to train personnel to work with culturally and linguistically different exceptional children (CLDE). In addition, both the Office of Special Education Programs (OSEP) and the Office of Bilingual Education and Minority Language Affairs (OBEMLA) of the U.S. Department of Education have funded research and training projects.

The Council for Exceptional Children has sponsored two national topical conferences and a symposium on this topic. As a result of these new developments, a body of information has emerged. In this monograph, five state-of-the-art papers on this important segment of our population have been prepared by some of the more prominent and active authorities in the area, adding significantly to our information base.

Philip C. Chinn
Professor and Head
Department of Special Education
East Texas State University
Commerce, Texas

Formerly Special Assistant to the
Executive Director for
Minority and Handicapped Concerns
The Council for Exceptional Children

CONTRIBUTORS

Leonard Baca, Director, BUENO Center for Multicultural Education, University of Colorado, Boulder

Philip Chinn, Professor and Head, Department of Special Education, East Texas State University, Commerce

Nancy Dew, Project Associate, New York Bilingual Education Multifunctional Support Center (NYBEMSC), Hunter College/Teachers College, Columbia University

Patricia Goldman, Research Associate, Vazquez-Nuttall Associates, Newton, Massachusetts

Patricia Medeiros Landurand, Senior Associate, Medeiros-Landurand Associates, Wayland, Massachusetts

Ena Vazquez Nuttall, Associate Professor, University of Massachusetts, Amherst

Alba Ortiz, Director, Bilingual/Special Education Programs, University of Texas at Austin

Robert Rueda, Associate Professor, Arizona State University, Tempe

CHAPTER 1

THE EXCEPTIONAL BILINGUAL CHILD: DEMOGRAPHY

Nancy Dew

The purposes of this investigative report are to document the prevalence[1] of exceptional bilingual children by handicapping condition, to analyze trends and patterns that present themselves in the available data, and to make recommendations for future data collection and monitoring efforts in regard to this specific population. Obtaining accurate prevalence figures enables educators to provide exceptional bilingual students with needed services and to modify those practices that prohibit access to services or improperly serve students. By analyzing the available data regarding enrollment, special educators can discover existing manpower planning and staff development needs and review the success of policies and programs developed to serve culturally and linguistically diverse exceptional (CLDE) students. In addition, funding levels can be established based on projections made with existing data.

DIFFICULTIES IN DETERMINING PREVALENCE RATES

Gathering accurate data regarding the number of exceptional children is complicated by several interacting variables. Factors identified by Hallahan and Kauffman in 1978 (pp. 8-12) included problems involving definition, diagnosis, sampling error, the role of the school, and stigma. A factor with special relevance to CLDE students is the tendency to use program placements other than special education classrooms to provide service. Typical of such placements are compensatory programs such as Title I (including Migrant programs), Title VII bilingual programs, and state and locally funded bilingual and English-as-a-second-language (ESL) programs.

---

[1]Prevalence refers to the number or percent of students who currently (or at a specified point in time) require special education services.

Definitions

Determination of the national prevalence rate of CLDE students in specific special education categories varies due to changing definitions for the various programs. In California, as in many other states, dramatic changes in enrollment rates were accomplished in the period 1969-1972, when large numbers of the state's EMH (educable mentally handicapped) students were decertified based on a court-mandated reassessment. Students were decertified because a greater weight was placed on performance IQ measures and because a lower IQ cutoff score was used (Meyers, Macmillan, & Yoshida, 1978; Reschly & Jepson, 1978).

While such changes in the category of mental retardation caused dramatic fluctuations in prevalence figures during this period, another more stable phenomenon is responsible for other fluctuations in the figures reported by states. This phenomenon is the considerable variation that exists among and within states in the definitions governing categorical programs. It is very much the case that a child's state and city of residence could determine whether a particular child is served and into which category the child is placed (U.S. General Accounting Office, 1981). In the high-incidence categories (educable mentally retarded, learning disabled, and speech impaired), due to the subjective criteria involved in their definitions, considerable variation in the characteristics and number of children served in the same categorical program exists among states (Hallahan & Kauffman, 1978; U.S. General Accounting Office, 1981). In 1980-81 the enrollment figures reported by states varied from a low of 4.81% to a high of 10.64% for the percentage of children classified and served in special education programs (General Accounting Office, 1981, p. 43).

As they regard CLDE students, the definitions of specific handicapping conditions have purposefully been refined over time to prevent misplacement or overrepresentation of such children. The most significant revisions made to the definitions of categorical programs are reflected in the intent and provisions of P.L. 94-142 (Ysseldyke, 1981). State provisions and court mandates specific to CLDE students have also caused the prevalence rates to change within and among categories in a similar fashion. While it is relatively easy to alter the placement rates for specific categories of exceptionality by changes made in the definitions regarding such programs, the key issue is not "numbers of cases," a standard open to active manipulation, but rather the validity of the placement and the equity that exists in the treatment of various ethnolinguistic groups within special education.

Diagnosis

It is possible that many students demonstrate overlapping conditions and are receiving the services of two categorical programs and yet are only reported under one. This would misrepresent actual service patterns in reporting districts. However, a more important issue for CLDE students is the accuracy of the diagnosis that places such students into the categories in which they are later reported. Assessment techniques have undergone a series of changes over the last decade, causing fluctuation in the actual diagnosis that places a child in a given category for reported purposes. A child who was reported as EMR at one point in time, using traditional testing procedures and strict cutoff points, might become learning disabled (LD) for another reporting period because the assessment procedure and the criteria used to diagnose the disability had changed.

A variety of sources documents the movement that occurs between categories as diagnoses change. Notably, there have been rather dramatic shifts away from placing CLDE children in EMR classrooms, and a continuing trend to serve students previously placed in these settings in LD or other compensatory classes (Finn, 1982; Jones-Booker, 1977; Tucker, 1980; U.S. General Accounting Office, 1981). Such shifts in figures reported will continue to occur as advances in the diagnosis of disabilities for this population occur. The advent of specialized training programs for bilingual psychologists and speech pathologists holds the promise of improved diagnosis of disabilities for limited-English-proficient youngsters and of increased accuracy in placements. The increased use of noncategorical programs may further affect prevalence figures.

Sampling Error

Studies that have been conducted thus far document prevalence in particular populations and then project these findings to larger populations. In this process, there always exists the potential for error. If the sample is too small, not representative, or skewed in a particular direction, the results will not predict accurately the number of students to be served. A related problem of great importance to the accurate prediction of CLDE students is that of the degree of disaggregation of data. One problem that exists in understanding the needs of this group is the lack of ethnic or national origin separation in the data currently collected. Hispanics, Asians, and Native Americans are grouped into large undifferentiated categories that do not allow program planners to understand the needs of particular groups of children. Distinctions such as Puerto Rican vs. Cuban vs. Mexican American children, Southeast Asian vs. Chinese vs. Filipino American children, or Navajo vs. Cherokee vs. Alaskan Native American children are but a few examples of the distinctions needed in order to adequately plan for the delivery of services.

Figure 1 and Table 1 show some of the broad divisions that would be necessary to provide accurate assessments, plan individualized education programs, and upgrade the skills and knowledge of the staff who would serve such children. Additionally, it would be necessary to distinguish among students with different proficiency levels in English and in their native languages in order to assess the need for native language services and personnel. These points are listed under sampling error because we know that our samples are not as carefully defined as they need to be in order for accurate statements to be made regarding current needs of CLDE children.

FIGURE 1

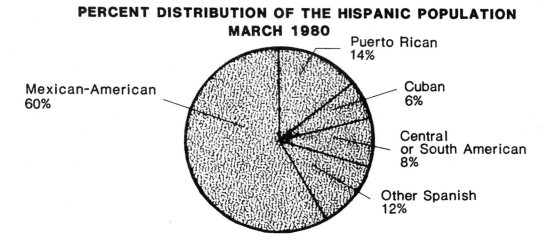

PERCENT DISTRIBUTION OF THE HISPANIC POPULATION
MARCH 1980

Puerto Rican
14%

Cuban
6%

Central
or South American
8%

Mexican-American
60%

Other Spanish
12%

Note. From the National Hispanic Center for Advanced Studies and Policy
Analysis. The State of Hispanic America: Volume II. Oakland: The
National Hispanic Center/BABEL, 1982, p. 6. Reprinted by permission.

TABLE 1
Languages Taught Most Frequently

Language	Number of Students enrolled	Percent of total
Total	31,338	100
Navajo	11,196	36
Cherokee	4,445	14
Dakota/Lakota	4,214	13
Papago	2,369	8
Other languages	22,224	29

Note. Information on services to American Indian and Alaskan Native
students comes from the BIA study reported in Comprehensive Indian
Bilingual- Bicultural Education Needs Assessment.
U.S. Department of Education. The Condition of Bilingual Education in the
Nation, 1982. Rosslyn: National Clearinghouse for Bilingual Education,
1982, p. 61.

4

The Role of the School

Schools assume a central role in the identification of students with handicapping conditions. While some disabilities are identified in infancy and early childhood, the most frequently occurring disability categories are tied to lack of school achievement. In the major studies conducted to document the number of students enrolled in special education, we can see that not only are students identified during their school years, but also that they are most frequently identified during the elementary school period. Data collected in the 1978-79 school year show that 57% of the students enrolled in special education were in grades 6 and below. The average age of children in special education was 8 years old (U.S. General Accounting Office, 1981). Concomitantly, the preschool, secondary, and postsecondary groups are underserved by special education programs. Other groups that do not receive adequate services are migrant children, foster children, incarcerated youth, and students enrolled in a variety of private school settings (U.S. General Accounting Office, 1981).

Another trend of great importance in the resultant prevalence rates is the trend to place students in existing programs in the district, rather than to create a needed new program. The number of "slots" open in programs has also been determined to influence the placements made (U.S. General Accounting Office, 1981). Enrollment prompted by the need to maintain staff and programs has been documented as well (Tobias et al., 1982). While these practices are not embraced by all special education programs, they are widespread enough to call into question the rates of enrollment that currently exist. Another issue related to the effect of the role of the school on resultant prevalence rates is the ability of staff to accurately distinguish between students in need of special education services and those whose needs can be met in the general education classroom.

While some researchers have documented the failure of general education programs to serve students as individuals (Tucker, 1980), others point to both a capricious referral practice by some educators and at the other extreme, the reluctance to refer demonstrated by others who feel that special education settings are not adequately constructed to serve CLDE students (U.S. General Accounting Office, 1981). The school plays a key role in who is served, the categorical programs in which they are served, and the trends of over-referral discussed above

Stigma

Because of an awareness of the stigma that can result from placements in certain categorical programs, many educators are reluctant to refer underachieving children. This reluctance may be even greater regarding the referral and placement of CLDE children, because of a history of documented misplacements of such children. Therefore, children who may genuinely need such services may not receive them because of a cautious posture on the part of some educators. Another factor that comes into play is the reaction of parents to certain placements. For parents coming from diverse cultural and linguistic backgrounds and educational experiences, there may be a general lack of understanding regarding the

5

purpose and content of special education classes. Because of this lack of understanding, parents may deny permission to have their child tested or in extreme cases they may even move in order to avoid the placement of their child in special education. Students who may need to be served in one category may be served in another because one is less stigmatizing than the other and is thus more readily accepted by parents. These are some of the many ways in which the possible stigmatizing effect of a program can affect the behavior of educators and parents as they make educational decisions. The illustrations given serve to demonstrate possible ways in which stigma can affect the resultant prevalence rates.

Alternative Placements/Programs

This section is very much related to the section on the role of the schools. It is being discussed separately, however, because of its importance to the prevalence rates reported for CLDE children. The existence of alternative programs in which underachieving students can be served dramatically affects the rates of participation in special education classrooms. For many students, alternative settings available are limited to Chapter I programs or school-developed compensatory programs. If a student is underachieving, the availability of such alternatives can affect whether or not the child is referred to special education. For CLDE students, a greater variety of program options can exist. These include migrant education programs (Title I funded), bilingual education programs (Title VII and state funded), and ESL classes (Title I and district funded), to name the most commonly available programs. Bilingual students who exhibit learning difficulties may be served in these settings rather than be referred to special education, thereby reducing the number of students reported as in need of special eduction services. Additionally, Title I basic skills programs (reading and mathematics) tend to be used as a "first placement" for students who are not succeeding in the general education classroom, be they monolingual special needs or bilingual youngsters who have exhibited a need for a bilingual program (McKay & Michie, 1982).

With the advent of P.L. 94-142, which required the provision of special education services to qualified students, the use of Title I programs for monolingual special needs students diminished. However, the use of Title I to provide language-related services to bilingual students has not diminished (McKay & Michie, 1982). By analyzing the data reported by the Office of Civil Rights in 1978 on a district-by-district basis, it can be seen that districts with bilingual programs have less disproportionality in their program enrollments than is the case in districts without bilingual programs. This suggests that students are served in special education settings to a greater extent when no bilingual program options exist (Finn, 1982). This fact raises questions as to whether bilingual students needing special education services are not being served and counted in special education settings when other program options exist, or whether students erroneously served in special education are better served in districts with Title I and bilingual program options. It is possible that both of these trends exist simultaneously, which would contribute to both underestimating and overestimating the numbers of CLDE students (Finn, 1982).

STUDIES DOCUMENTING THE NUMBERS AND CHARACTERISTICS
OF CLDE STUDENTS IN THE UNITED STATES

The studies reported here cover the period 1978 through 1983 in order to be relevant to educators currently planning services for CLDE students. Three broad areas are covered: national studies, state-by-state studies, and LEA (local school district) studies. In each of these sections, issues that emerge regarding the target student population or regarding data collection efforts are discussed. In the interest of brevity, issues are presented under only one of the three major divisions, even though the issues could pertain equally to all of the studies reported. Readers who wish a more comprehensive analysis of the data are referred to the original sources which contain a wealth of information regarding the target group.

National Studies

Two major national studies are conducted at regular intervals to determine the prevalence of children receiving special education services. They are the Office of Civil Rights (OCR) survey, conducted biannually, and the Office of Special Education Programs (OSEP) Child Count, conducted annually. Each of these studies has a different purpose. The OCR study is conducted primarily to assess compliance of LEA's (local education agencies) with civil rights statutes, and the OSE study is conducted to determine P.L. 94-142 funding levels for states, based on reported and projected child counts. There are differences in the counts obtained by these two surveys, with the OSEP child count almost 23% higher than the OCR totals. Differences in the figures obtained by the two efforts are generally attributed to the differences in purpose, data collection methods, timing of the data collection, and reporting content and procedures (U.S. Accounting Office, 1981). While at the district level it is acknowledged that the OCR counts may be underestimates and while no assurances exist that the OSEP child count data are entirely accurate either, in general, confidence is placed in the findings of these surveys.

Based upon these two major national studies, a summary of the numbers and characteristics of children served in special education is presented here. This summary proceeds from characteristics that apply to the entire special education population to those that apply specifically to the CLDE subgroup.

In the 1980-81 school year, 10.08% of the estimated 3- to 21-year-old population were reported as receiving special education and related services. This is well below the number anticipated in 1974 by the Office of Special Education prior to the enactment of P.L. 94-142, despite major efforts on the part of all states to locate students who qualify for services. As a result, there are many who question the original 12% estimate proposed by the OSEP (U.S. General Accounting Office, 1981). As previously stated, based on data gathered in 1980-81, the actual prevalence rates that existed in states ranged from a low of 4.81% in New Hampshire to a high of 10.64% in Utah (U.S. General Accounting Office, 1981). Program planners who attempt to project the population of CLDE students in need of special education services using school enrollment or census figures and multiplying by expected prevalence rate need to bear this variation in mind when projecting such figures. The 12% rate seems unjustifiably high and program planners might do well to use the existing local rate, rather than this predicted national rate, which has never been realized. Using 1981-82 figures, the national proportion of children served as handicapped was reported at 10.47%, remaining fairly stable compared to the previous year's rate of 10.08% (U.S. Dept. of Education, 1983).

In the fall of 1978, figures were compiled regarding the numbers of students served in special education by racial/ethnic breakdown. Table 2 demonstrates that while white students were 75% of the national enrollment they were only 71% of the special education population. Black students made up 16% of the national enrollment and 21% of the special education population. Hispanics comprised 7% of the national enrollment and 6% of the special education population, and Asian American and Native Americans comprised approximately 1% of both the national and special education enrollments nationwide.

Based on the OCR survey conducted in 1978, it is also apparent that males are over-represented in special education settings. They are 3 times as likely to be placed in programs for the seriously emotionally disturbed and 2 1/2 times as likely to be placed in classes for the learning disabled as girls; they are also over-represented in classes for the mentally retarded in significant proportions. This phenomenon is uniform across geographic regions and tends to become more aggravated in lower SES districts (Finn, 1982; Heller, 1982; U.S. Accounting Office, 1981).

As has already been described, 67% of the handicapped students are 12 years of age or younger; the mean age is 8. Overall, the enrollment figures demonstrate that the preschool, secondary, and postsecondary groups are under-served by special education programs (U.S. General Accounting Office, 1981).

A significant negative relationship exists between racial disproportion and socioeconomic status (SES) for each minority group except Asian or Pacific Islanders. The relationship is strongest for Native American and Alaskan native students, and least strong for students of Hispanic origin. That is, in districts with lower SES populations, the disproportionate enrollment of minority students was greater than in higher income districts (Finn, 1982).

Data regarding the enrollment of children in specific special education programs across ethnic/racial groups is reported in Tables 3, 4, and 5. These tables represent figures collected by the Office of Civil Rights in 1978 and 1980. It is important to note the different ways in which data are reported, making it difficult to contrast trends over time without returning to the original sources to convert the data to the same format for analysis. Yet all of these tables (two for 1978 and one for 1980) demonstrate differing patterns of under- and over-enrollment for each ethnic/racial group in the different categorical programs.

TABLE 2

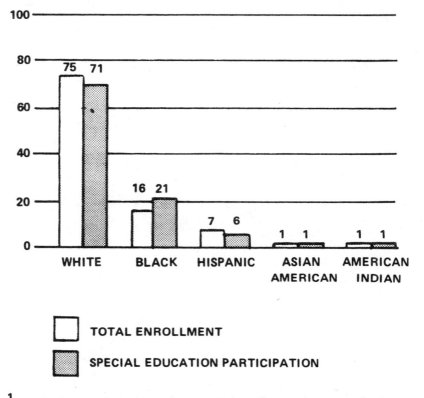

DISTRIBUTION OF CHILDREN ENROLLED IN ELEMENTARY
AND SECONDARY SCHOOLS BY RACE-ETHNICITY AND
DISTRIBUTION OF CHILDREN PARTICIPATING IN SELECTED
EDUCATION PROGRAMS BY RACE-ETHNICITY DURING THE
SCHOOL YEAR 1978-1979 (IN PERCENTS)[1,2]

[1] SOURCE: FALL 1978 ELEMENTARY AND SECONDARY SCHOOLS CIVIL
RIGHTS SURVEY

[2] SELECTED SPECIAL EDUCATION PROGRAMS INCLUDED THOSE FOR
THE EDUCABLE MENTALLY RETARDED, TRAINABLE MENTALLY
RETARDED, SERIOUSLY EMOTIONALLY DISTURBED, SPECIFIC
LEARNING DISABLED, AND SPEECH IMPAIRED.

Note. From U.S. General Accounting Office. <u>Disparities still exist in
who gets special education.</u> (Report by the Comptroller General to the
Chairman, Subcommittee on Select Education, Committee on Education and
Labor, House of Representatives of the United States; Report IPE-81-1)
Washington, D.C.: U.S. General Accounting Office, Sept. 30, 1981, p. 32.

TABLE 3
Nationwide Special Education Placements for Specific Racial or Ethnic Groups

Student Group	American Indian/ Alaskan Native	Asian/ Pacific Island	Hispanic	Black	White
Percentage of Student Population[a]	.79	1.42	6.75	15.72	75.32
Percentage in Special Education Programs:[b]					
Educable Mentally Retarded (EMR)	1.73	.37	.98	3.46	1.07
Trainable Mentally Retarded (TMR)	.23	.15	.24	.39	.19
Seriously Emotionally Disturbed (SED)	.33	.10	.29	.50	.29
Specific Learning Disabilities (SLD)	3.49	1.27	2.58	2.23	2.32
Speech Impaired (SI)	1.87	1.85	1.78	1.87	2.04

Note. From Finn, J.D. (1982). Patterns in special education placement as revealed by the OCR survey. In Heller, K.A., and others, Placing children in special education: Equity through valid educational practices. Final report. ERIC Document Reproduction Service No. ED 217 618, p. 55.
[a]From State, Regional, and National Summaries of Data from the 1978 Civil Rights Survey of Elementary and Secondary Schools, prepared for the Office of Civil Rights by Killalea Associates, Inc., April 1980. On estimated total school enrollment of 41,836,257 students.
[b]Percentages are based on weighted projects to national totals from 1978 OCR survey data.

TABLE 4
Department of Education, Office for Civil Rights
1980 Elementary and Secondary Schools Civil Rights Survey
National Summary of Reported Data

Student Group	Am In	Asian	Hisp	Black	Minority	White	Total	Male	Female	Hand	IEP
Enrollment:											
Number	199,144	638,085	2,573,628	5,718,590	9,129,607	19,366,847	28,496,454	14,616,530	13,878,730	2,390,245	771,867
Percent	0.7	2.2	9.0	20.1	32.0	68.0	100.0	51.3	48.7	8.4	2.7
Expulsions:											
Number	1,172	271	10,813	23,174	35,430	60,623	95,953	67,982	37,942	2,111	N/A
% of Total	1.2	0.3	11.3	24.2	36.9	63.1	100.0	70.8	29.1	2.2	N/A
P. Rate[a]	5.9	0.4	4.2	4.1	3.9	3.1	3.4	4.7	2.0	0.9	N/A
Suspensions:											
Number	8,582	11,295	129,912	575,888	725,677	968,332	1,684,009	1,164,324	526,355	45,012	N/A
% of Total	0.5	0.7	7.7	34.2	43.1	56.9	100.0	69.1	31.3	2.7	N/A
P. Rate[a]	43.1	17.7	50.5	100.7	79.5	49.5	59.1	79.7	37.9	18.8	N/A
Corp. Punishment:											
Number	5,679	2,201	61,998	336,507	406,385	621,633	1,027,918	824,941	202,944	34,079	N/A
% of Total	0.6	0.2	6.0	32.7	39.5	60.5	100.0	80.3	19.7	3.3	N/A
P. Rate[a]	28.5	3.4	24.1	58.8	44.5	32.1	36.1	56.4	14.6	14.3	N/A
Gifted/Talented:											
Number	2,657	34,112	42,616	87,081	166,466	617,706	784,141	377,683	406,809	N/A	N/A
% of Total	0.3	4.4	5.4	11.1	21.2	78.8	100.0	48.2	51.9	N/A	N/A
P. Rate[a]	13.3	53.5	16.6	15.2	10.2	31.9	27.6	25.8	29.3	N/A	N/A
EMR:											
Number	3,461	1,997	19,404	181,816	206,678	194,615	401,293	241,394	159,817	N/A	4,536
% of Total	0.9	0.5	4.8	45.3	51.5	48.5	100.0	60.2	39.8	N/A	1.1
P. Rate[a]	17.4	3.1	7.5	31.8	22.6	10.0	14.1	16.5	11.5	N/A	5.9
TMR:											
Number	554	1,028	6,433	23,070	31,085	44,371	75,456	42,989	32,332	N/A	1,581
% of Total	0.7	1.4	8.5	30.6	41.2	58.8	100.9	57.0	42.8	N/A	2.1
P. Rate[a]	2.8	1.6	2.5	4.0	3.4	2.3	2.6	2.9	2.3	N/A	2.0
Speech Impair.:											
Number	3,657	10,011	45,223	117,111	176,002	443,645	619,647	391,656	228,103	N/A	13,501
% of Total	0.6	1.6	7.3	18.9	28.4	71.6	100.0	63.2	36.8	N/A	2.2
P. Rate[a]	18.4	15.7	17.6	20.5	19.3	22.9	21.7	26.8	16.4	N/A	17.5

Continued on page 12

TABLE 4 (Continued)

Ser. Emot. Dist.:										
Number	1,022	637	10,802	42,634	55,095	94,191	116,089	149,286	32,656	1,424
% of Total	0.7	0.4	7.2	28.6	36.9	63.1	77.8	100.0	21.9	1.0
P. Rate[a]	5.1	1.0	4.2	7.5	6.0	4.9	7.9	5.2	2.4	1.8
Spec. Learn Dis.:										
Number	7,863	9,046	76,026	176,548	263,483	621,750	643,490	891,233	247,532	14,572
% of Total	0.9	1.0	8.5	19.8	30.2	69.8	72.2	100.0	27.8	1.6
P. Rate[a]	39.5	14.2	29.5	30.9	29.5	32.1	44.0	31.3	17.8	18.9
Bilingual:										
Number	11,165	102,709	525,049	6,073	40,022	644,996	N/A	685,018	N/A	N/A
% of Total	1.6	15.0	76.6	0.9	5.8	94.2	N/A	100.0	N/A	N/A
P. Rate[a]	45.7	84.2	50.1	74.8	47.4	62.8	N/A	69.7	N/A	N/A
Graduates:										
Number	9,096	34,558	102,419	286,250	432,323	914,441	967,038	1,861,412	N/A	39,120
% of Total	0.5	1.8	5.4	15.2	23.0	48.6	51.4	100.0	N/A	2.1
P. Rate[a]	84.2	39.8	50.1	74.8	47.4	62.8	69.7	65.0	N/A	16.5

Special Ed:	2,608,417		Restrictive Policy For		Schools With Accessible	
Special Ed:	2,567,557		Pregnant Students:	577	Entrances:	35,923
Elsewhere:	144,575		Medical Cert Only:	540	Restrooms:	26,292
Evaluated:	144,516		Separate Programs:	2,768	Science Labs:	10,708
Receiving Services:	14,724		Mandatory Programs:	126	Pupils in Wheelchairs:	27,807
					Accessible Classrooms:	838,326
					Total Classrooms:	1,353,227

	Single Sex Classes		Mixed Classes			Males	Females	Teams
	Males	Females	Males	Females				
Home Economics	11,710	311,126	604,676	1,026,544	All Female Teams		1,450,687	86,952
Industrial Arts	357,239	8,736	1,342,206	595,436	All Male Teams	2,572,204		118,438
Physical Ed	1,033,757	941,386	3,966,077	3,645,380	Teams Both Sexes	210,685	129,192	21,183

Note. From DBS Corporation. (1982, March). 1980 elementary and secondary schools civil rights survey: National survey. ERIC Document Reproduction Service No. ED 219 477, p. 12.

[a]P. Rate = Participation rate, which is rate per thousand.

TABLE 5

Distribution Of Children Receiving Special Education By
Nature Of Handicapping Condition And Race/Ethnicity,
School Years 1978-79   (In Percents)

Handicapping condition	American Indian	Asian American	Black	White	Hispanic
Educable mentally retarded	22.6[a]	10.0	41.0	18.1	16.7
Trainable mentally retarded	3.0	4.1	4.7	3.3	4.0
Emotionally disturbed	4.4	2.7	6.0	5.0	5.0
Learning disabled	46.0	34.0	26.3	39.2	44.0
Speech impaired	24.0	49.3	22.1	34.5	30.2
Totals[b]	100.0	100.1	100.1	100.1	99.9

Note. From Fall 1978 Elementary and Secondary School Civil Rights
Surveys. U.S. General Accounting Office, 1982, p. 62.
Note. Figures are in percentages. Analysis is limited to the five
handicapping conditions presented.
[a]Interpret as 22.6 percent of all American Indian students who were in
special education in school year 1978-79 were in an educable mentally
retarded program.
[b]Totals may not sum to 100 due to rounding.

Within the categorical programs it is important to notice that 85% of all children receiving special education are served in three categories: learning disabilities, speech impairments, and mental retardation. Programs for learning disabled students enrolled 36% of the special education students, for the speech impaired enrolled 30% of the students, and for the mentally retarded enrolled 19% of the students. It was also reported in the OSE 1980-81 data that 51% of children in special education have mild handicaps, 36% have moderate handicaps, and 13% have severe handicaps (U.S. General Accounting Office, 1981).

In its Fifth Annual Report to Congress on the implementation of P.L. 94-142, the Office of Special Education Programs of the U.S. Department of Education reported increases in the numbers of students served in the categories of learning disabled, emotionally disturbed, and multihandicapped children. In the categories of speech impaired, mentally retarded, other health impaired, deaf and hard of hearing, and orthopedically and visually handicapped students, decreased numbers were reported. Growth in the LD category between the period of 1977-78 to 1981-82 assumed the tremendous proportion of 104% (U.S. Department of Education, 1983). In 1980-81, in six states learning disabled students made up more than 50% of all handicapped students served; in 12 additional states they comprised more than 40% of the children served (U.S. General Accounting Office, 1981). Such trends are important backdrops against which to study the patterns of under- and over-enrollment presented regarding CLDE children.

An interesting finding that emerges in the data is that there are specific characteristics exhibited by districts where disproportionate enrollment is great. Two important characteristics that correlate to disproportionate enrollment are the size of the district and the racial composition of the district. These issues are explored here using national studies, but might be equally valid regarding state and local data presented later in this paper.

In general the data of large districts obscure that of smaller districts when figures are collected for examination on a state-by-state basis. Smaller districts examined separately typically demonstrate characteristics not common to their urban counterparts. In small school districts there are problems caused by the presence or absence of certain categorical programs. For example, while the degree of disproportion in EMR placement is directly related to the size or existence of EMR programs, in general in small school districts the disproportion in EMR minority placements is particularly large and may be in need of in-depth federal investigation (Heller, 1983).

Another interesting trend emerges in districts based on size of the district and percentage of minority enrollment. Among medium-sized and large districts, as the percentage of minority enrollments increases, disproportionate enrollment decreases. In contrast, in small districts with more than 50% minority enrollments, there is evidence of increased disproportions. Possible causes for such trends would include differences in assessment and placement procedures, differences in definitions used in categorical programs, and the availability of facilities and resources other than special education to service minority students (Finn, 1982).

Another interesting finding is that districts with the highest disproportion levels have the smallest proportion of students in bilingual programs (Finn, 1982). It is possible, therefore, that students in need of bilingual programs are misclassified in special education when no bilingual programs are available to serve them. For large districts with high Hispanic enrollment, 78% have bilingual education programs available. In such districts, the lowest disproportions in EMR and SLD programs are seen for Hispanic students (Finn, 1982). Tables 6 and 7 demonstrate how the rates of enrollments in different categorical programs vary as the minority composition of the school varies. Without such disaggregation of data, it would be impossible to truly understand the patterns of enrollment that exist among districts in their special education programs.

Trends can also be isolated by geographic locale, since programs with greater percentages of certain minority populations are found in particular regions of the country. Such is the case for students of Asian or Pacific Island origin who nationally are enrolled in special education programs at rates considerably below those for whites. However, in small districts in several western states, positive disproportions are found in the enrollment figures. By comparison, Hispanic students are placed in EMR settings at rates close to those for nonminority students in California and New York in districts of all sizes. In Arizona, Colorado, and New Mexico, two patterns exist: Small or negative disproportions exist when the percentage of Hispanic students enrolled in the district is below 50%. However, when the enrollment figure for Hispanics reaches 70% or more, EMR disproportion is high. In Texas, the disproportion is relatively large in all districts with 10% or more Hispanic students and small among districts with smaller Hispanic enrollment (Finn, 1982; Heller, 1982).

The above discussion demonstrates that district size, geographic location, and percentage of minority enrollment interact in various ways and produce trends that merit further study to determine their exact cause. Other district characteristics that could be correlated to enrollment patterns to determine the kinds of relationships that exist include the availability of minority diagnostic and instructional staff, the policies and practices that demonstrate administrative support for the equitable treatment of ethnolinguistic minority students, the degree of community or legal pressure applied to particular school districts, and the rural, suburban, and urban distinctions that could be drawn among districts.

TABLE 6
Department of Education, Office For Civil Rights
1980 Elementary and Secondary Schools Civil Rights Survey
National Summary of Reported Data
Participation in Gifted/Talented Programs By Percent Minority Composition of School

Gifted/Talented Programs		Minority Composition of School				
		0-20%	20-40%	40-60%	60-80%	80-100%
Member:	Minority	17,298	22,429	30,389	31,060	65,290
	Non-Minority	349,370	144,244	82,646	32,100	9,345
Participation Rate:	Minority	19.0	15.0	19.1	22.3	17.5
	Non-Minority	26.2	40.4	50.6	52.6	46.1

Note. From DBS Corporation. (1982, March). 1980 elementary and secondary schools civil rights survey: State summaries. Volume I. ERIC Document Reproduction Service No. ED 219 478, p. 18.

TABLE 7
Department of Education, Office for Civil Rights
1980 Elementary and Secondary Schools Civil Rights Survey
National Summary of Reported Data
Special Education Program Participation by
Percent Minority Composition of School

Special Education Group		Minority Composition of School				
		0-20%	20-40%	40-60%	60-80%	80-100%
Total Special Education						
Number:	Minority	92,659	158,863	143,858	106,776	236,187
	Non-Minority	954,438	260,385	118,780	45,724	19,245
P. Rate[a]:	Minority	101.6	106.5	90.4	76.6	63.1
	Non-Minority	71.5	72.9	72.7	74.9	94.9
EMR						
Number:	Minority	23,064	47,354	42,420	27,921	65,929
	Non-Minority	132,865	34,009	16,991	7,141	3,609
P. Rate[a]:	Minority	25.3	31.8	26.6	20.0	17.6
	Non-Minority	10.0	9.5	10.4	11.7	17.8
TMR						
Number:	Minority	2,711	5,714	6,876	6,135	9,649
	Non-Minority	24,675	9,914	5,975	2,578	1,229
P. Rate[a]:	Minority	3.0	3.6	4.3	4.4	2.6
	Non-Minority	1.8	2.8	3.7	4.2	6.1
Speech Impaired						
Number:	Minority	22,679	35,067	33,832	25,759	58,665
	Non-Minority	306,947	80,708	37,081	13,749	5,160
P. Rate[a]:	Minority	24.9	23.5	21.3	18.5	15.7
	Non-Minority	23.0	22.6	22.7	22.5	25.4
Seriously Emotionally Disturbed						
Number:	Minority	5,914	10,357	10,193	7,847	20,784
	Non-Minority	59,289	18,842	9,985	3,844	2,231
P. Rate[a]:	Minority	6.5	6.9	6.4	5.6	5.6
	Non-Minority	4.4	5.3	6.1	6.3	11.0
Specific Learning Disabled						
Number:	Minority	38,301	60,371	50,637	39,114	81,160
	Non-Minority	430,662	116,912	48,748	18,412	7,016
P. Rate[a]:	Minority	42.0	40.5	31.7	28.1	21.7
	Non-Minority	32.3	32.7	29.9	30.1	34.6

Note. From DBS Corporation. (1982, March). <u>1980 elementary and secondary schools civil rights survey: State summaries.</u> Volume II. ERIC Document Reproduction Service No. ED 219 479, p. 19

[a]P. Rate = Participation rate, which is rate per thousand.

State-by-State Reports of CLDE Students

The reports presented in this section include the office of Civil Rights State Summaries of Reported Data for the year 1980 (DBS Corporation, 1982), and special studies that analyze trends in the states of California, Colorado, Florida, Massachussetts, Texas, and New Jersey. The issues considered here include the trend toward placing ethnolinguistic minority students in LD rather than EMR programs, the disproportions that exist across ethnic groups in programs for the gifted and talented, and the variation in treatment received by CLDE students depending on the geographic locale and specific internal characteristics of the district in which they are served.

Table 8 presents a summary of states where the Hispanic population makes up 1% or more of the state's total population. It can be seen that for five of the states listed, Hispanics represent more than 10% of the state's population. For four additional states, the percentage exceeds 5% of the state's total population. Because of their relative ranking as states with high Hispanic population totals, and in order to give some variety in terms of geographic location, information from the 1980 OCR study is presented for the states of California, Colorado, Texas, Illinois, New York, Massachusetts, and Florida (Table 9).

General Trends. A surface analysis of the 1980 data suggests that for the states selected, proportional or over-enrollment in gifted and talented programs is the case with White and Asian students. This pattern is somewhat modified in Colorado, New York, and Massachusetts where Blacks also appear to be more proportionately enrolled. In general, Asian students, who tend to be over-enrolled in programs for the gifted and talented, tend to be under-enrolled in the other categories. In states where this is not the case, a higher enrollment of Asian students also exists in the category of speech impaired. Since the numbers of Native American students are small, it is difficult to discuss trends for this group. Hispanics tend to be under-enrolled in programs for the gifted and talented, and over-enrolled in classes for the mentally retarded. There are some exceptions to this pattern in the states selected, notably Illinois and Florida. While not of principal interest in this study, it appears to be still very much the case that the greatest disproportions in enrollment in special education classrooms exist for Black students (with the exception of Massachusetts).

These tables, or those of the 1982 OCR survey, would provide excellent sources from which to construct in-depth analyses such as that conducted by Finn in 1982. It is unfortunate that such analyses are not routinely carried out for the benefit of educators serving CLDE students, but are dependent on the interest and dedication of individual researchers.

TABLE 8
States Ranked According to Hispanic Population

State	Rank	Hispanic Population	Hispanic % of State Total	% of U.S. Hispanic Population
California	1	4,543,770	19.2	31.1
Texas	2	2,985,643	21.0	20.4
New York	3	1,659,245	9.5	11.4
Florida	4	857,898	8.8	5.9
Illinois	5	635,525	5.6	4.4
New Jersey	6	491,867	6.7	3.4
New Mexico	7	476,089	36.6	3.3
Arizona	8	440,915	16.2	3.0
Colorado	9	339,300	11.7	2.3
Michigan	10	162,388	1.8	1.1
Pennsylvania	11	154,004	1.3	1.1
Massachusetts	12	141,043	2.5	1.0
Connecticut	13	124,499	4.0	.9
Washington	14	119,986	2.9	.8
Ohio	15	119,880	1.1	.8

Note. From U.S. Department of Commerce News, July 17, 1981 CB81-118 as cited in The National Hispanic Center for Advanced Studies and Policy Analysis, 1982, p. 7.

TABLE 9
Department of Education, Office for Civil Rights
1980 Elementary and Secondary Schools Civil Rights Survey
Special Education Program Participation by
Percent Minority Composition of State

State	American Indian	Asian	Hispanic	Black	White
California					
% of enrollment	.8	7.1	26.1	11.9	64.7
" G/T	.4	10.8	9.8	6.6	72.4
" EMR	.7	2.5	28.7	24.4	43.7
" TMR	.5	5.2	27.3	15.8	51.3
" S/I	.5	4.9	26.0	9.2	59.4
" ED	.5	1.5	19.9	29.2	48.9
" SLD	.8	1.7	21.9	12.9	62.8
Colorado					
% of enrollment	.6	1.9	15.3	5.4	76.9
" G/T	.4	3.0	15.2	9.0	72.5
" EMR	.7	.7	22.3	12.3	64.1
" TMR	.2	1.5	20.2	4.1	74.0
" S/I	.4	2.2	16.1	4.5	76.8
" ED	.6	.5	11.2	10.2	77.5
" SLD	.4	.6	15.6	6.9	76.5
Texas					
% of enrollment	.2	1.2	30.0	16.6	52.0
" G/T	.1	1.7	15.7	11.2	71.3
" EMR	.1	.3	30.0	38.5	31.1
" TMR	.1	.4	36.6	25.2	37.7
" S/I	.1	.7	27.0	15.4	56.8
" ED	.1	.2	17.5	16.4	65.7
" SLD	.1	.2	30.7	19.6	49.3

TABLE 9 Continued

State	American Indian	Asian	Hispanic	Black	White
Illinois					
% of enrollment	.1	1.7	8.4	29.6	60.2
" G/T	.1	2.2	3.7	18.9	75.2
" EMR	.4	.6	4.2	58.8	35.9
" TMR	.7	.9	7.5	33.6	57.3
" S/I	.3	2.4	5.7	20.7	70.8
" ED	1.7	.5	4.5	35.7	57.5
" SLD	.3	.9	5.1	24.2	69.6
New York					
% of enrollment	.2	2.4	18.4	20.9	57.1
" G/T	.3	6.6	13.4	23.5	56.1
" EMR	.2	.5	17.3	38.1	43.8
" TMR	.1	1.6	24.3	32.3	41.6
" S/I	.3	1.6	8.2	15.1	74.9
" ED	.1	.3	22.0	48.1	29.4
" SLD	.2	.7	11.6	21.5	66.0
Massachusetts					
% of enrollment	.1	1.4	4.8	9.1	84.6
" G/T	.1	2.8	2.8	9.9	84.3
" EMR	.1	.4	6.2	5.4	87.8
" TMR	.0	1.1	3.2	1.1	94.6
" S/I	.0	1.0	2.3	2.0	94.7
" ED	.3	.3	3.7	4.7	91.0
" SLD	.1	.2	2.1	2.5	95.2
Florida					
% of enrollment	.1	.8	8.0	23.1	68.0
" G/T	.0	1.3	1.5	3.2	94.0
" EMR	.1	.1	3.5	63.7	32.7
" TMR	.1	.4	7.8	35.3	56.4
" S/I	.1	.7	4.9	29.7	64.7
" ED	.1	.2	2.9	33.6	63.4
" SLD	.1	.2	6.9	29.2	63.7

Note.   From DBS Corporation, 1980.   Elementary and secondary school civil rights survey: State summaries.   Volume I of II.   ERIC Document Reproduction Service No. ED 219 478, March, 1982.

Analysis of Selected States in the 1980 OCR Survey and Other State Studies

California. Various studies conducted in California attest to the movement that occurred in the period 1968-1974 when large numbers of students previously enrolled in EMH programs were documented as being served instead in EH (educationally handicapped) classes (Jones-Booker, 1977; Meyers, Macmillan, & Yoshida, 1978) (see Figure 2). Others report that while earlier serious over-enrollment problems existed for Hispanic students in special education classrooms, based on current data, Hispanics are now seriously under-represented. The shift from over-enrollment to under-enrollment is attributed to current legislation in California (A.B. 1870), which requires all districts to submit incidence figures as a part of their Master Plans to eliminate the "retarded" category (Pacheco, 1983).

Florida. According to a report issued in April 1982, Hispanic students comprise 7.99% of the preschool through 12th grade population in Florida. In some school districts in Florida, Hispanic students comprise even greater percentages of the school enrollment. In Dade County they make up 37.63% of the student population; in Hardee, 19.26%; in Collier, 19.09%; in Hendry, 13.91%; and in Monroe, 13.01%. When statewide percentages of Hispanics are compared with special education enrollments, a pattern of under-enrollment emerges in all programs except the TMR program, where they are more proportionately enrolled (State of Florida, 1982). Since the data presented is aggregated for the entire state, it isn't possible to analyze trends that may present themselves in those counties with greater Hispanic enrollment listed above. No figures were provided for other language groups. This data is very similar to the data provided in the 1980 OCR survey, and it is presumed that these are the actual figures submitted for that survey.

Massachusetts. In June of 1978, the Massachusetts Advocacy Center released its report <u>Double Jeopardy: The Plight of Minority Students in Special Education</u>. In this report, it was demonstrated that minority enrollment rates in special education were significantly different from the enrollment rates of nonminority students, that minority students were disproportionately placed in the most restrictive programs, and that minority students were under-represented in special day and residential prototypes. In their third report on the status of those districts first cited, issued in December 1980, it was reported that four of the nine school districts originally cited were no longer demonstrating disproportionate placements. Signs of progress were also reported in the other five districts, where attempts were under way to remedy the situation (Massachusetts Advocacy Center, 1980). This effort to overcome the reported prima facie denial of Hispanic and Black students' rights was also the focus of a presentation made at the February 1981 Conference on the Exceptional Bilingual Child (McDonnell, 1981). In the remedial plans submitted, most of the original districts cited proposed programs that would review the placement of minority students, hire bilingual/bicultural staff, provide inservice training, refine assessment procedures, increase program alternatives available, improve the instructional environment in special education classrooms, and make

FIGURE 2

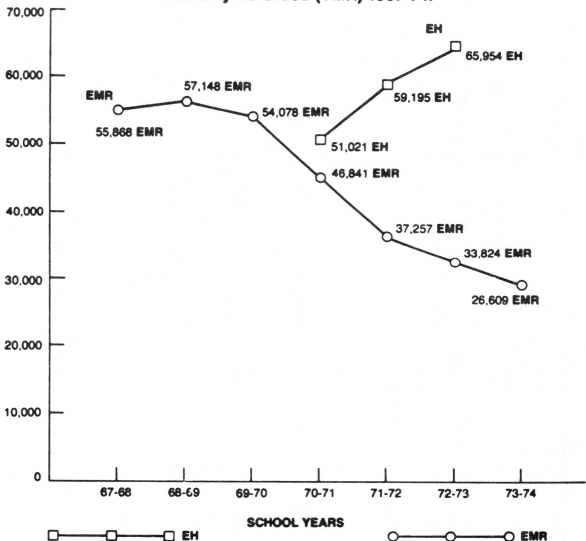

A Comparison of Educable Mentally Retarded (EMR), Educationally Handicapped (EH) and Trainable Mentally Retarded (TMR) 1967-74.

Note. From Jones-Booker, R. Evaluation of educable mentally retarded programs in California. (A report prepared by the California Advisory Committee to the U.S. Commission on Civil Rights). ERIC Document Reproduction Service No. 144 326, May, 1977, p. 11.

additional efforts to involve and train parents. A surface analysis of the OCR data reported in 1980 seems to support the findings of the third report of the Massachusetts Advocacy Center. While these OCR figures represent all districts in the state and not just the districts cited, one could argue, based on the two studies, that monitoring efforts initiated in Massachusetts seem to be producing the desired results. The role that monitoring can play in achieving education equity is discussed later in this report.

New Jersey. In a report issued by the New Jersey State Department of Education in November 1980 the following findings were reported:

1. Within the state of New Jersey a disproportion exists between White and racial/ethnic minority students in the classification of children as handicapped.

2. This disproportion is primarily found in the EMR and ED classifications, with Hispanics and Blacks having a higher representation.

3. Many individual school districts evidence excessive rates of disproportion that cannot be explained by unique local conditions.

4. Low SES students have an increased chance of being labeled as EMR.

5. The assessment practices used with minority youngsters were cited as contributing to the disproportionate enrollments found.

Data used for this study were collected in a survey covering the period 1979-1980. Evidence of disproportionate enrollment in other categorical programs for minority groups is also given in this study (Manni et al., 1980).

LEA (Local Education Agency) Studies

According to a report issued by the U.S. Department of Commerce News on July 17, 1981, there are 25 cities in the United States with Hispanic populations of 50,000 or more (The National Hispanic Center for Advanced Studies and Policy Analysis, 1982). These cities are located in 10 states: Arizona, California, Colorado, Florida, Illinois, New Jersey, New Mexico, New York, Pennsylvania, and Texas (see Table 10). Because of the magnitude of the task of reporting on enrollment patterns in individual districts in the U.S., three districts have been selected to serve as examples, those ranking first, second, and third in terms of their Hispanic population figures. Additionally, a report that identified 100 cities with disproportionate minority enrollment based on 1978 OCR data will be briefly reviewed.

TABLE 10
25 Cities with Hispanic Populations of 50,000 Or More

Rank	Cities	Population
1	New York	1,405,957
2	Los Angeles	815,989
3	Chicago	422,061
4	San Antonio	421,774
5	Houston	281,224
6	El Paso	265,819
7	Miami	144,087
8	San Jose	140,574
9	San Diego	130,610
10	Phoenix	155,572
11	Albuquerque	112,084
12	Dallas	111,082
13	Corpus	107,908
14	Hialeah	103,175
15	Denver	91,937
16	Santa Ana	90,946
17	Laredo	85,076
18	San Francisco	83,373
19	Tucson	82,189
20	Brownsville	71,139
21	Austin	64,766
22	Philadelphia	63,570
23	Newark	61,254
24	Fresno	51,489
25	Long Beach	50,700

Note. From U.S. Department of Commerce News, July 17, 1981 CB81-118 as cited in The National Hispanic Center for Advanced Studies and Policy Analysis, 1982, p. 8.

LIBRARY
ATLANTIC CHRISTIAN COLLEGE
WILSON, N. C.

85- 1750

New York City. As can be seen in Table 10, New York City ranks first in Hispanic population in the United States. Hispanics have been documented as comprising 40% of the handicapped children in the city (Linares, 1983). In a report issued in July 1980, which used October 1979 data, the following findings were generated about New York City enrollments: (a) While specific districts demonstrated disproportionate representation for those students referred to special education, citywide referrals were ethnically proportionate; (b) Hispanics were under-represented in SLD Resource Room Programs; and (c) Hispanics were the most severely under-represented group in private school placements for EH and EMR students (Tobias et al., 1980). These findings were again demonstrated in a report issued in March 1982 (Tobias et al.). These reports point to the need to collect data on a district-by-district basis rather than citywide, the need to look at public versus private school enrollment by ethnic group, and the need to study enrollment by program type and to analyze the possible reasons students are under-represented (e.g., lack of staff to provide certain types of programs).

Los Angeles. Limited data sources were located specific to Los Angeles, although unquestionably such data exists in quantity. In the OCR data reported in 1978, several patterns of disproportionate enrollment were apparent. These patterns are highly similar to the national trends of under- and over-enrollment of Asian and Hispanic students reported earlier (Killalea Associates, Inc., 1978). Using data from the same year, the Los Angeles Division of Special Education issued a compliance plan that described its intent to improve services delivered to LES/NES (limited- and non-English-speaking) students in the district. The plan defines assessment procedures, program development efforts, staff hiring and training efforts, and parental involvement efforts that would be undertaken to improve the disproportionate enrollment pattern that existed at the time for LES/NES students within the Division of Special Education (Los Angeles Unified School District, 1979). Using Los Angeles as an example, the need to compare enrollment figures not only on the basis of ethnic/racial composition, but also on the basis of language proficiency levels is demonstrated. In this manner it is possible to respond to evaluation, programming, staffing, and parental needs based on linguistic needs.

Chicago. Ranking third in Hispanic population in the nation, Chicago also demonstrates serious disproportionate enrollment patterns. Compared with White students, Hispanic students were consistently under-represented in special education, only half as likely as White students to get special education services at all. Chicago also demonstrated the pattern seen in New York City, where there were huge variations from one administrative district to another and from one school to another in terms of referral and placement rates. Even though the rates of enrollment for Hispanics were notably low, there were still questions raised regarding whether or not students were appropriately placed and served (Designs for Change, 1982) (Figure 3). Three reasons were cited as causes for the Hispanic under-representation: the use of bilingual

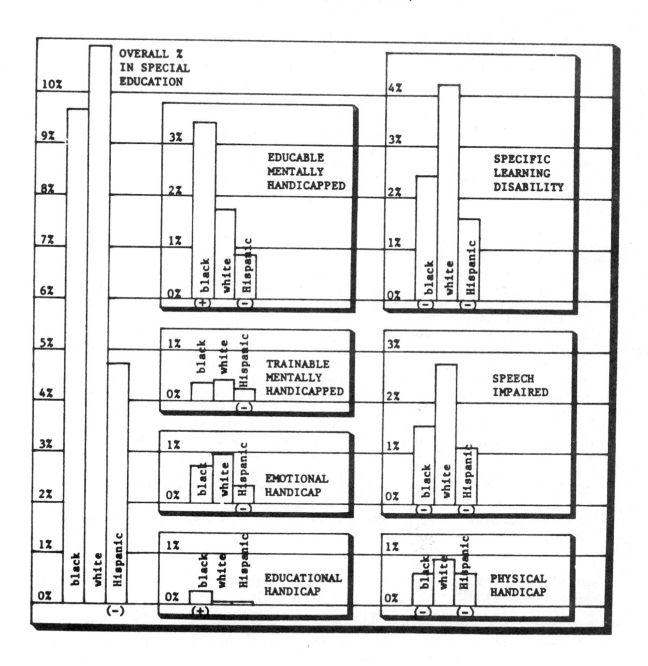

FIGURE 3
Rates of Participation in
Various Special Education Programs
in Chicago by Ethnic Group
(1980-81 School Year)

Note. From Designs for Change. Caught in the web: Misplaced children in Chicago's classes for the mentally retarded. ERIC Document Reproduction Service No. 231 910, December, 1982. p. 27. Reprinted by permission.

27

education programs to serve Hispanic handicapped children, the lack of bilingual special education teachers, and the existence of administrative directives designed to discourage the referrals of LEP Hispanic students to special education (Designs for Change, 1982). Since this report does not disaggregate limited-English-proficient (LEP) from English-proficient Hispanic students, it is difficult to substantiate the causes cited in explaining the under- enrollment pattern. However, since 1981 substantial efforts have been under way in Chicago to document the need for specialized services to be developed and delivered to limited-English-proficient (LEP) Hispanic students. Using the October, 1982 special education count taken, it was documented that 2,311 LEP handicapped students were enrolled in special education classrooms citywide. These students came from 38 non-English-language backgrounds. Hispanics constituted 88% of the population (2,030 students), the second largest population was Italian (41 students), and the next 10 language groups ranged from 33 to 11 students per language group. Due to the clear domination of Hispanic students in Chicago's LEP population, specific efforts have been under way to improve service delivery to this group.

In 1982, 38 Spanish-speaking teachers were identified as currently holding special education positions in the district. It was documented at that time that an additional 58 such teachers were required to serve the reported population. In addition, there was a need for small numbers of special education teachers speaking Italian, Arabic, Vietnamese, Korean, and Assyrian. Eight districts in the city accounted for 83% of the LEP handicapped population, with 21% enrolled in a single district. Learning disabilities teachers made up 47% of the bilingual special education staff and EMH teachers made up 22% (Benavides, 1983). Chicago's efforts in collecting data specific to the needs of the LEP handicapped population serve as a very useful model for other districts to follow. This interest in specialized data collection initially pointed to improvements needed in the reporting techniques used. Once an accurate accounting of students was accomplished, the patterns that emerged were very useful for program planning and staff development efforts. An additional procedure worth noting is the use of a local prevalence rate to predict and monitor enrollment patterns, rather than the use of a national figure. All of the comparisons and predictions made in Chicago use a 10.58% prevalency rate (local rate) rather than 12% (predicted national rate) as is commonly used in many studies (Benavides, 1984).

Disproportionate Representation Of Limited-English-Speaking/Non-English Speaking (LES/NES) Pupils

Using OCR data collected in 1978, a special summary was accomplished which listed and ranked 100 districts in the nation which most appear to warrant investigation for discrimination in the disproportionate placement of LES/NES pupils. Of these districts, the proportion of LEP students enrolled in special education classes ranged from 7% to 100%.

Sixteen districts had all of their limited-English-proficient (LEP) students enrolled in special education settings. More than 40 of the cited districts had 50% or more of their LEP students in special education classes. While actual numbers of LEP students in a given district may have been small, this apparent indiscriminate use of special education classes to serve LEP students warrants further investigation (Killalea Associates, 1978). Such information is useful to program planners and improves on the reporting of data purely by ethnic/racial categories which masks the needs of the LEP subpopulation. This report could have far greater impact if the data were analyzed, if follow-up monitoring in the cited districts were accomplished, and if the findings were made available to interested educators.

SPECIAL EXCEPTIONAL BILINGUAL STUDENT POPULATIONS

In this section a brief summary of published information is provided for the following groups: Native American, migrant, preschool, and LEP handicapped students. Readers with a special interest in any of these groups are referred to the original sources for a more comprehensive treatment of the issues briefly summarized here.

American Indian Exceptional Students

Table 1 provides data regarding the language groups served in Bilingual/Bicultural programs for American Indian and Alaskan Native students in 1981. As can be seen in this chart, while some language groups are reported separately, the bulk of this population is listed in an undifferentiated category. Projecting needs for this group is complicated by such reporting procedures. When attempting to consider the needs of the handicapped within this larger population, few resources could be located that provided such information. While by no means comprehensive or representative of all American Indian populations, the Annual Report of the Bureau of Indian Affairs (BIA) Advisory Committee for Exceptional Children, which lists the number of handicapped children receiving special education and related services by category in BIA schools, is one of the few published documents available regarding a portion of this population. Table 11 provides this data for the years 1980 and 1981.

As can be seen in these tables, large numbers of children are served in three categories: mentally retarded, speech impaired, and learning disabled. The LD category serves more than half of the students enrolled in special education settings. The so called "hard" categories of physical or sensory impairments have very low enrollments. These findings deserve comprehensive analysis to determine the causes for such patterns. The relatively low identification of deaf and hearing impaired children deserves special attention due to the prevalence of hearing loss for this group documented by Stewart (1983). In addition to this limited report, several sources were located that document staffing patterns. In general these sources point to the need for staff, and specifically the need for American Indian special education personnel, to properly serve existing populations of students (Anderson & Anderson, 1983; BIA Advisory Committee for Exceptional Children, 1981, 1982; Fracek, 1981, 1982;

TABLE 11
Bureau of Indian Affairs
Projected December FY 1980 Child Count

AREAS	Mentally Retarded	Hard of Hearing	Deaf	Speech Impaired	Visually Impaired	Seriously Emotionally Disturbed	Orthopedically Impaired	Other Health Impaired	Specific Learning Disability	Multi-Handicapped	Deaf/Blind	TOTAL
Aberdeen	87	9	1	355	4	8	9	6	375	10	1	865
Albuquerque	30	2	0	57	0	3	3	0	183	20	0	298
Anadarko	11	0	0	7	0	0	0	1	36	0	0	55
Billings	13	5	0	32	0	5	1	1	55	0	0	112
Eastern	73	1	1	53	0	22	0	7	144	3	0	304
Juneau	47	4	1	16	0	2	0	2	194	5	0	271
Minneapolis	5	4	0	49	0	2	3	2	25	3	0	93
Muskogee	1	0	0	0	0	0	0	0	14			15
Navajo	195	93	0	201	19	106	12	3	1021	122	0	1772
Phoenix	34	0	0	48	2	40	2	2	237	17	0	382
Portland	12	15	0	50	0	6	1	0	97	3	0	184
Institutionalized	104	0	9	1	0	30	2	0	7	120	0	273
Total	612	133	12	869	25	224	33	24	2388	303	1	4624

**Number of Handicapped Children Receiving
Special Education and Related Services**

(December 1981 Child Count)

AREAS												
Aberdeen	127	10	4	446	2	36	6	8	455	20	1	1115
Albuquerque	15	2	0	56	0	2	2	0	138	24	0	239
Anadarko	8	0	0	12	0	2	0	0	86	0	0	108
Billings	4	5	0	14	0	13	0	0	51	2	0	89
Eastern	65	2	1	52	0	22	5	6	158	2	0	313
Juneau	43	7	0	15	1	3	0	1	193	8	0	271
Minneapolis	4	0	0	75	0	7	0	1	56	2	0	145
Muskogee	2	0	0	0	0	0	0	0	13	0	0	15
Navajo	239	62	1	184	9	68	10	3	1013	71	0	1665
Phoenix	34	0	0	51	1	50	1	0	282	13	0	432
Portland	16	4	0	37	0	7	1	5	111	2	0	183
Institutionalized	179	0	8	0	0	53	0	0	0	43	0	283
TOTAL	736	92	14	942	13	263	25	24	2561	187	1	4858

Note. Sources:
Bureau of Indian Affairs, Advisory Committee for Exceptional Children. The second annual report to the Department of the Interior. Washington, D.C.: U.S. Dept. of the Interior, Office of Indian Education Programs, November 1981.
Bureau of Indian Affairs, Advisory Committee for Exceptional Children. The third annual report to the Department of the Interior. Washington, D.C.: U.S. Dept. of the Interior, Office of Indian Education Programs, November 1982.

Ramirez & Tippeconnic, 1979). Two South Dakota studies point to a serious special education over-enrollment problem in that state, with 17-18% of American Indians enrolled in special education versus an 11% school enrollment rate (Fracek, 1981, 1982). These studies also document that American Indian staff make up only 1.5% of the "full-time" employees for schools which have a combined rate of American Indian student enrollment of 11%.

Gathering complete data for this population hinges on first accurately defining who is considered American Indian and then gathering comprehensive data in a variety of education settings, including public schools, BIA schools, and residential facilities, as well as out-of-school youngsters aged 3-21. The need for such data is critical.

Migrant Exceptional Students

Migrant students are a significantly underserved group in regard to special education and related services (Serrano, 1982; U.S. General Accounting Office, 1981). Assessing data is extremely problematic for this population of students. In many states no figures are available to show the number of migrant handicapped students, but in those with data, the figures suggest serious under-representation problems.

In a special issue of Exceptional Children (April 1982), various authors pointed out the plight of migrant exceptional students. Frith explained that while it is difficult to estimate the number of students in need of service, it is likely that the number is disproportionately high due to psychosocial disadvantages, minimal emphasis on migrant education in many localities, and limited continuity in educational programming. Perry stated that there is no accurate count of students identified or eligible for services, the types and relative frequency of handicapping conditions are unknown, the count of students being served is not known, and the types of service being received by those served are also not well-documented. Baressi proposed that the reasons migrant handicapped children are not identified are because many children are never enrolled in school, because they drop out early, or because their teachers do not become familiar with their needs due to sporadic attendance and frequent changes in enrollment. Mobile handicapped children may move before they are placed in a program even when assessment is accomplished, and those who are assessed may not be adequately assessed due to language and culture barriers. Phecha and Ward found that of those students identified, more tended to demonstrate serious or obvious conditions and thus were more likely to be referred. It was also noted that the development and transmission of IEP's caused problems in providing a continuous and appropriate education program to such students even if identified and placed. The combined findings of the sources given paint a picture of a group which is underidentified, poorly assessed, which receives inadequate programming, lacks continuity in services, and which may eventually drop out of school entirely. Figures for this group are almost nonexistent.

Preschool Exceptional Children

As stated earlier in this report, preschool children constitute one of the underserved groups principally because the bulk of services are aimed at elementary school children. Not all preschool children attend a preschool or day care program. Those who do participate in a variety of settings including public school programs, private day care and preschool programs, or Head Start programs, to name a few. Thus gathering data on this group would require compiling any existing figures from all of these settings.

As with the American Indian handicapped population, one source regularly published which permits some analysis of trends regarding this population is the Annual Report to the Congress of the U.S. Department of Health and Human Services regarding services provided to handicapped children in Head Start programs. In its eighth annual report (1981), it was reported that 12% of children enrolled in Head Start programs in 1980 were handicapped. Of these, approximately 59% were speech impaired; 12% were health impaired; 7% were emotionally disturbed; 6% were mentally retarded, orthopedically handicapped, or learning disabled; 4% were hearing impaired, and 3% were visually impaired. Less than 5% were deaf or blind (U.S. Dept. of Health and Human Services, 1981). This report also documented that 8.70% of students enrolled in Indian Programs and 6.91% of those enrolled in migrant programs had been identified as handicapped. In the ninth annual report these percentages had risen to 10.41% in Indian programs and 11% in migrant programs (U.S. Dept. of Health and Human Services, 1983). Since Section 13(e) of the Economic Opportunity Act of 1964, as amended (P.L. 93-644), requires that no less than 10% of the total enrollment in Head Start programs be handicapped students, the total percentage of students reported is not as meaningful as the separation of that population into the different categories. Other than the Indian and migrant subdivisions, we have no idea what proportion of the total population reported as handicapped are CLDE children. This report does confirm, however, the high proportion of children identified as speech impaired, a statistic also documented in OSEP data (U.S. Dept. of Health and Human Services, 1981). This tendency to identify large percentages of handicapped preschool children as speech impaired, as compared to the school aged handicapped population which has half this percentage served in the speech impaired category, warrants futher examination. Particular interest could be paid to the Head Start setting where the mandate to serve a certain percentage may increase the identification of children as speech impaired.

Services at the preschool level, while not adequately defined, do point to a need to ensure that diagnostic and instructional staff are adequately trained to identify disabilities and to intervene with CLDE children.

Limited-English-Proficient Exceptional Students

As was seen in the analysis of LEA data, some efforts have been made to collect information regarding the number of LEP students in special education settings. However, typically we have no idea what range of proficiency is represented in the LEP category. Studies that report on LEP students need to specify the criteria used to define proficiency levels, the range of proficiency considered LEP, the native language ability of LEP students reported, and ethnic background of reported LEP students. Such refinements in the way data is reported could provide more usable information to program planners.

A major study that provides information on the LEP population in the United States is the Children's English and Services Study conducted by J. Michael O'Malley (1981, 1982). Other general sources that have reported on the number of non-English-language background and LEP students include a study by Oxford, Pol, Lopez, Stupp, Gendell, and Peng (1981) and census information gathered in 1980 (Knerr, 1982; Waggoner, 1982). While these studies have been used by educators to gather baseline data upon which to make projections of the numbers of handicapped LEP children of particular categories, they provide no concrete information regarding CLDE children. Thus, it is unfortunate that the bulk of studies regarding LEP students do not report on disabled LEP students, and the bulk of reports generated to document the numbers of handicapped children do not report effectively about the LEP subgroup.

Several studies and reports were located that do provide information regarding the LEP handicapped group. The data reported earlier on Chicago is such a study. Three other studies were located. Two of these studies were conducted in California.

In May of 1983 the National Center for Bilingual Research issued a report entitled <u>Communication Disorders in Limited and Non-English Proficient Children</u>, conducted by Linda Carpenter. The major findings of this report are as follows:

1. Approximately 20% of the children served by the survey respondents were reported to be LEP/NEP, which contradicts district level data suggesting that LEP/NEP communicatively disordered children comprised less than 1% of the students served.

2. The types of disorders demonstrated by LEP/NEP communicatively disordered students were of the same type and frequency as those in the general Communicatively Impaired (CI) population.

3. Speech clinicians have noted an increase in the number of LEP/NEP students in need of speech and language services in the last 3 to 5 years.

4. The presence of bilingual education programs influences speech and language services received.

Of the LEP/NEP students served, 82.71% were of Spanish language background, 13.70% were of Asian language background, and 3.59% were of other language backgrounds.

A more comprehensive study of LEP students was recently completed by Cegelka, Rodriguez, Lewis, Pacheco, and Santa Cruz, of the San Diego State University (1984). This report examines current state practices in educating handicapped LEP students of 11 disability types. The report generates information regarding the presentation of LEP students in special education, the prevalence of LEP in special education settings as compared to the total school population, the prevalence of LEP students by handicapping category, and the prevalence of identification as handicapped for each of six language subgroups. The only significant differences found in this study were in the case of prevalence of LEP under the categories of SED and Other Health Impaired. For all other categories, while differences were found, they were not significant. The prevalence of handicapping conditions was documented as 11.08% for LEP students and 8.01% for the general student population, while the prevalence of limited English proficiency was reported as greater among the general school population (11.01%) than among the handicapped population (7.36%). The study gathered information on district practices relative to identification, screening, assessment, IEP development, and program placement as well as on due process procedures, parent participation, and perceived teacher inservice training needs. A second portion of the study focused on the identification of promising practices in the educational service delivery for handicapped LEP students. The findings of this study and the recommendations made for future research concerning the LEP handicapped population promise to be very useful to educators planning programs for CLDE students, especially along qualitative lines.

A final study located was one conducted by Gilbert L. Delgado in 1980 concerning hearing impaired children with non-native home languages. This study found that an estimated 7% of children from non-English-speaking homes in the U. S. were hearing impaired. Of the programs surveyed, 40% reported at least one child from a non-English-speaking home. Of the group of children from non-English-speaking homes, 51% had additional handicaps. The study also reports on numbers of hearing impaired children from outside the U. S., and documents instructional practices implemented with the students in the programs surveyed. While the study does document that the numbers of hearing impaired children from non-native-language homes are increasing, important information regarding the proficiency of the students is missing. Due to lack of communication with the home, respondents were often not certain of the language spoken there, so this information is also lacking. However, a total of 21 languages other than English were reported, the predominant language being Spanish, followed by Portuguese, Vietnamese, and several East Indian languages and dialects. A contribution made by the study is the delineation of specific areas in which research is needed regarding this population under the broad categories of assessment, language, culture, and demography.

In summary, various studies do exist that provide information about the LEP handicapped population. All of the studies conducted thus far have limitations. Those that point to specific needs for future research have made important contributions in defining the scope and nature of such efforts.

MONITORING THE DELIVERY OF SERVICES TO CLDE STUDENTS: RECOMMENDED PRACTICES

By collecting accurate and comprehensive data regarding the CLDE population, more fruitful monitoring activities could take place. These would include analyzing the accuracy of referrals of CLDE students made by classroom teachers, the ability of current assessment practices and personnel to diagnose disabilities for the CLDE group, the accuracy of placements made for CLDE students, the effectiveness of instructional services delivered, and the adequacy of programs and staff selected to meet the specific needs of CLDE students. Monitoring efforts conducted thus far have been undertaken by the Office of Civil Rights, community action groups, court actions, or the result of state or district self-checks initiated due to the desire to understand service patterns.

Monitoring recommendations made in the documents used for this report include the following (Benavides, 1984; Designs for Change, 1982; Jones-Booker, 1977):

1. School districts should collect and analyze information regarding the number of referrals to special education by language proficiency level, within each ethnic group by individual attendance center. Such disaggregation is sorely needed in the data reported.

2. School districts should report the numbers of CLDE placements in various special education programs by type of placement (resource room, private school placement, etc.). Effectiveness of placements should be monitored, especially those that are more restrictive.

3. The state education agency (SEA) should conduct an investigation in any school system that demonstrates disproportionate patterns of minority enrollment, both for the possible misclassification of children and the adequacy of services received.

4. The SEA should create positive incentives (i.e., funding) for the school districts to classify and serve CLDE children accurately.

5. Districts should develop special administrative policies that encourage solutions to problems of misclassification and disproportionate enrollment for CLDE students.

6. SEA staff responsible for monitoring programs should be representative of the populations they serve. Minority representation in such staffs is important.

7. Monitoring efforts need to take place on site, not through reports. Follow-up visits are recommended. Funding for these activities should be provided.

8. Enforcement procedures need to be developed. Financial control is suggested.

9. When students are moved out of a categorical program, special efforts should be undertaken to monitor treatment and progress.

10. Transition from a bilingual/ESL program to the general education classroom is an important juncture to study. Many bilingual students are referred to special education at this time of transition.

11. Emphasis should be on providing prereferral solutions in the general education or bilingual classroom; in addition, districts should provide training to educators regarding how to identify ethnolinguistic minority students in need of referral.

REFERENCES

Anderson, G. R., & Anderson, S.K. (1983) The Exceptional Native American In D. R. Omark & J. G. Erickson (Eds.), The bilingual exceptional child (pp. 163-180). San Diego: College-Hill Press.

Baressi, J. G. (1982) Educating handicapped migrants: Issues and options. Exceptional Children, 48(6), 473-488.

Benavides, A. (1983). Summary regarding the number of handicapped limited-English proficient students and special education staff serving such students. Unpublished report.

Benavides, A. (1984). Personal Communication, December, January.

Bureau of Indian Affairs, Advisory Committee for Exceptional Children. (1981). The second annual report to the Department of the Interior. Washington, DC: U.S. Department of the Interior, Office of Indian Education Programs.

Bureau of Indian Affairs, Advisory Committee for Exceptional Children. (1982). The third annual report to the Department of the Interior. Washington, DC: U.S. Department of the Interior, Office of Indian Education Programs.

Carpenter, L. (1983). Communication disorders in limited- and non-English proficient children. Los Alamitos: National Center for Bilingual Research.

Cegelka, P. T., Rodriguez, A., Lewis, R.B., Pacheco, R., & Santa Cruz, R. (1984). Special education services for LEP handicapped students: State of the art and future directions. Specially prepared annotation of project findings. San Diego State Univ. (Study to be released, Spring, 1984)

DBS Corporation. (1982). <u>1980 elementary and secondary schools</u>
<u>civil rights survey, National Survey</u>. ERIC Document
Reproduction Service No. ED 219 477.

DBS Corporation. (1982). <u>1980 elementary and secondary schools</u>
<u>civil rights survey: State summaries. Volume I</u>. ERIC Document
Reproduction Service No. ED 219 478.

DBS Corporation. (1982). <u>1980 elementary and secondary schools</u>
<u>civil rights survey: State summaries. Volume II</u>. ERIC
Document Reproduction Service No. ED 219 479.

Delgado, G. L. (1980). <u>International baseline data on hearing</u>
<u>impaired children with non-native home languages</u>. Unpublished
manuscript, Gallaudet College.

Designs for Change. (1982). <u>Caught in the web: Misplaced children</u>
<u>in Chicago's classes for the mentally retarded</u>. ERIC Document
Reproduction Service No. 231 910.

Finn, J. D. (1983). Patterns in special education placement as
revealed by the OCR survey In K. A. Heller et al., (Eds.),
<u>Placing children in special education: Equity through valid</u>
<u>educational practices. Final report</u>. ERIC Document
Reproduction Service No. ED 217 618, pp. 551-617.

Fracek, E. E. (1981). <u>Office of Indian Education survey results:</u>
<u>Indian self-identified certified staff (ISICS), Fall 1981</u>.
South Dakota State Division of Elementary and Secondary
Education. ERIC Document Reproduction Service No. ED 230 331.

Fracek, E. E. (1982). <u>Office of Indian Education survey results:</u>
<u>Indian self-identified certified staff (ISICS), Fall 1982</u>.
South Dakota State Division of Elementary and Secondary
Education. ERIC Document Reproduction Service No. ED 230 332.

Frith, G. H. (1982). Educating immigrant students: The
paraprofessional component. <u>Exceptional Children,</u> <u>48</u>(6),
506-507.

Hallahan, D. P., & Kauffman, J. P. (1978). <u>Exceptional children:</u>
<u>Introduction to special education</u>. Englewood Cliffs: Prentice
Hall.

Heller, K. A. (1982). <u>Placing children in special education:</u>
<u>Equity through valid educational practices. Final report</u>. ERIC
Document Reproduction Service No. ED 217 618. (Also available
from National Academy Press, Washington, D.C.)

Jones-Booker, R. (1977). <u>Evaluation of educable mentally retarded</u>
<u>programs in California</u>. (A report prepared by the California
Advisory Committee to the U.S. Commission on Civil Rights).
ERIC Document Reproduction Service No. ED 144 326.

Killalea Associates, Inc. (1978). 1978 elementary and secondary schools civil rights survey: Analysis of selected civil rights issues. Volume I, Reports on ranked districts for the nation. ERIC Document Reproduction Service No. ED 185 215.

Knerr, Wilbur. Breakdown of Asian and Pacific Island; American Indian, Eskimo and Aleut; and Spanish Origin school age children by state-1980. Three tables based on 1980 census data, mailed December 1983 by request. Rosslyn: National Clearinghouse for Bilingual Education.

Linares, N. (1983). Management of communicatively handicapped Hispanic American children. In D. R. Omark & J. G. Erickson (Eds.), The bilingual exceptional child. San Diego: College-Hill Press.

Los Angeles Unified School District Division of Special Education. (1979). Law Compliance Plan for Division of Special Education Students.

Manni, J. L., and others. (1980). The status of minority group representation in special education programs in the state of New Jersey: A summary report. (New Jersey State Dept. of Education #PTM-100.83). ERIC Document Reproduction Service No. ED 203 575.

Massachusetts Advocacy Center. (1980). Double jeopardy: The plight of minority students in special education. Status report, number 3. ERIC Document Reproduction Service No. ED 203 636.

McDonnell, J. R. (1981). A systems approach for ameliorating possible prima facie denial of Hispanic/Black students' rights through disproportionate enrollment in special education. Paper presented at the Conference for the Exceptional Bilingual Child, New Orleans, February 19, 1981.

McKay, M. & Michie, J. (1982). Title I services to students eligible for ESL/bilingual or special education programs. (A special report from the Title I district practices study.) McLean: Advanced Technology, Inc.

Meyers, C. E., Macmillan, D. L., & Yoshida, R. K. (1978). Validity of psychologists' identification of EMR students in the perspective of the California decertification experience. Journal of School Psychology, 16(1), 3-15.

National Clearinghouse for Bilingual Education. (1982). 1980 Census shows 60% increase in Hispanic population. Forum, 5(2), 5.

National Clearinghouse for Bilingual Education. (1982). Detailed census data available from NCBE. Forum, 5(6), 3, 7.

The National Hispanic Center for Advanced Studies and Policy
   Analysis. (1982). The state of Hispanic America: Volume II.
   Oakland: The National Hispanic Center/BABEL.

O'Malley, J. M. (1981). Children's English and services study.
   Language minority children with limited English proficiency in
   the United States. Rosslyn: National Clearinghouse for
   Bilingual Education.

O'Malley, J. M. (1982). Children's English and services study.
   Educational needs assessment for language minority children with
   limited English proficiency. Rosslyn: National Clearinghouse
   for Bilingual Education.

Oxford, R., Pol, L., Lopez, D., Stupp, P., Gendell, J., & Peng, S.
   (1981). Projections of non-English language background and
   limited English proficient persons in the United States to the
   year 2000: Educational planning in the demographic context.
   NABE Journal, 5(3), 1-30.

Pacheco, R. (1983). Bilingual mentally retarded children: Language
   confusion or real deficits? In D. R. Omark & J. G. Erickson
   (Eds.), The bilingual exceptional child (pp. 231-253). San
   Diego: College-Hill Press.

Perry, J. (1982). The ECS Interstate Migrant Education Project.
   Exceptional Children, 48(6), 496-500.

Pyecha, J. N., & Ward, L. A. (1982). A study of the implementation
   of Public Law 94-142 for handicapped migrant children.
   Exceptional Children, 48(6), 490-495.

Ramirez, B. A. & Tippeconnic, J. W. (1979). Preparing teachers of
   American Indian handicapped children. Teacher Education and
   Special Education, 2(4), 27-32.

Reschly, D. J., & Jepson, F. J. (1976). Ethnicity, geographic
   locale, age, sex, and urban-rural residence as variables in the
   prevalence of mild retardation. American Journal of Mental
   Deficiency, 81(2), 154-161.

Serrano, V. Z. (1982). Migrant handicapped children: A second
   look at their special education needs. Denver: Education
   Commission of the states.

State of Florida, Department of Education. (1982). A resource
   manual for the development and evaluation of special programs
   for exceptional students. Volume III-B. Evaluating the
   non-English speaking handicapped. Tallahassee: State of
   Florida, Department of Education.

Stewart, J. L. (1983). Communication disorders in the American Indian population. In D. R. Omark & J. G. Erickson (Eds.), The bilingual exceptional child (pp. 181-195). San Diego: College-Hill Press.

Tobias, R., et al. (1980). The ethnic representation of special education referrals classifications and placements in New York City. Evaluation report. ERIC Document Reproduction Service No. ED 209 270.

Tobias, R., et al. (1982). Project referral, evaluation, and placement training, 1980-1981, Title VI-D. Final evaluation report. System design requirements for the child assistance program for the Division of Special Education, New York City Board of Education (NYC-OEE-5001-62-16601). ERIC Document Reproduction Service No. ED 221 980.

Tucker, J. A. (1980). Ethnic proportions in classes for the learning disabled: Issues in nonbiased assessment. The Journal of Special Education, 14(1), 93-105.

U.S. Department of Education. (1982). The condition of bilingual education in the nation, 1982. Rosslyn: National Clearinghouse for Bilingual Education.

U.S. Department of Education. (1983). To assure the free appropriate public education of all handicapped children. (Fifth annual report to Congress on the implementation of Public Law 94-142: The Education for all Handicapped Children Act) Washington DC: U.S. Department of Education; U.S. Office of Special Education and Rehabilitative Services..

U.S. Department of Health and Human Services, Administration for Children, Youth and Families. (1981). Eighth annual report to Congress on the status of handicapped children in Head Start Programs. Washington DC: U.S. Dept. of Health & Human Services.

U.S. Department of Health and Human Services, Administration for Children, Youth and Families. (1982). Ninth annual report to Congress on the status of handicapped children in Head Start Programs. Washington DC: U.S. Dept. of Health & Human Services.

United States General Accounting Office. (1981). Unanswered questions on educating handicapped children in local public schools. (Report to the Congress of the United States; HRD-81-43) Washington DC: U.S. General Accounting Office.

United States General Accounting Office. (1981). <u>Disparities still exist in who gets special education</u>. (Report by the Comptroller General to the Chairman, subcommittee on Select Education, Committee on Education and Labor, House of Representatives of the United States; Report IPE-81-1.) Washington DC: U.S. General Accounting Office.

Waggoner, D. (1982). 1980 Census language data and estimates of language minority and limited English proficient children and adults in the United States. <u>NABE News</u>, <u>5</u>(5), 5-6.

Ysseldyke, J. E. (1981). Foreword in T. Oakland (Ed.), <u>Nonbiased assessment</u>. Minneapolis: The National School Psychology Inservice Training Network.

CHAPTER 2

A CRITICAL LOOK AT TESTING AND EVALUATION
FROM A CROSS-CULTURAL PERSPECTIVE

Ena Vazquez Nuttall
Patricia Medeiros Landurand
Patricia Goldman

This paper attempts to define and describe the target population and discuss the common problems in distinguishing a "disability" from a cultural or linguistic difference. The legal mandates impacting on the assessment of linguistically and culturally different students are summarized. A brief summary and review of the research on the uses and misuses of standardized assessment instruments are presented; in addition, the most common approaches being practiced in the field of nondiscriminatory assessment are described and critically analyzed. Viable alternative nondiscriminatory assessment and evaluation techniques, approaches, and recommended model practices are recommended. Finally, recommendations in the area of cross-cultural assessment and evaluation will be made for local, state, and federal educators who are involved in either the development of policies or the implementation of services to culturally and linguistically different students who may or may not have exceptional needs.

WHO IS OUR TARGET POPULATION?

This paper focuses on a group of children identified as linguistically and culturally different, children who are native speakers of a language other than English. It includes both children from immigrant families and children from native-born American families who speak languages other than English. In defining this population, it must be remembered that in identifying a child as a member of a particular language group, one must not separate the language from the particular cultural context in which it is spoken. Different cultures may share a common language and yet vary greatly in cultural values: French-speaking children from Haiti, Canada, and France, for example, represent very different cultural and linguistic populations.

Therefore, although the term <u>linguistic minority student</u> refers to a student who is a native speaker of a language other than English, within this category there is wide diversity. The term may refer on one hand to those students of varying degrees of literacy who have just migrated with their families to the United States; to students who are living in the United States and learning both languages simultaneously; to second generation students who prefer to speak English at school and their native languages at home; and finally, to migrant children who may be represented in any of the above descriptions.

The term <u>culturally and linguistically different exceptional children</u> is defined as those individuals who exhibit discrepancies in growth and development due to health-related impairments, hearing impairments, mental retardation, orthopedic-related handicaps, serious emotional disturbances, learning disabilities, speech impairments, or visual impairments (Advisory Board of Access, 1981). The linguistic levels of these children would fall at varying points on a continuum. At one end of the continuum are the monolingual speakers of the first language (L_1). Then we have the dominant-L_1 speakers who have some English ability. In the middle of the continuum are the apparently bilingual students with comparable proficiency in both languages. Many of our exceptional students fall within the middle of this continuum as "semilinguals." A child defined as a semilingual is a child who is displaying equally poor ability in both languages. This kind of student is unable to perform cognitive tasks in either language. According to Cummins (1976), the threshold level of language development needed to function academically has not been reached by this child. Next on the continuum are the English-dominant students with some L_1 ability. Finally there are the monolingual-English students.

Although categorical definitions have often served to label students, isolate them, and deny them equal access to educational programs, a brief description of each of the major categories is useful.

The first widely used category is that of mental retardation. According to the American Association of Mental Deficiency (AAMD):

> Mental retardation refers to signficantly sub-average general intellectual functioning existing concurrently with deficits in adaptive behavior and manifested during the developmental period. (Grossman, 1977)

In this definition, "intellectual functioning" refers to results of individual intelligence tests and "significantly sub-average" refers to an IQ score more than two standard deviations below the mean. "Adaptive behavior" refers to the degree to which the individual meets personal independence and social responsibility expected of his or her age and cultural group (Grossman, 1977).

The socioeconomic and cultural and linguistic bias of standardized tests, particularly IQ tests, has led to questioning the value of using these tools with limited-English-proficient students as well as with other cultural and linguistic minority students (Cole, 1981; Laosa, 1977; Oakland & Matuszek, 1977; Olmedo, 1981).

Mercer (1973) discovered that of those persons who would have been labeled mentally retarded if their classification depended solely on test scores, a full 84% had completed eight grades or more in school, 83% had held a job, 80% were financially independent or housewives, and almost 100% were able to do their own shopping or travel alone.

Culturally and linguistically different students are most affected by the process of standardized testing. Unfamiliar test content, attitudes of examiners who may be unfamiliar with the child's culture, the students' limited proficiency in English, language variations, unfamiliarity with test conditions, and lack of motivation to perform well on the test are all critical factors that influence a student's performance on standardized tests. Therefore, the label "mentally retarded," traditionally arrived at through intelligence tests, is a very misused classification with linguistic, cultural, and racial minority students.

A second exceptional category is the behaviorally disordered. According to Rhodes and Tracy (as cited in Ambert & Dew, 1982), characteristics of behaviorally disordered students fall into two categories: hyperactive-aggressive and fearful-withdrawn. Some characteristics that appear in many definitions include an inability to learn that cannot be explained by other factors, difficulty in relating to others, inappropriate behavior under normal circumstances, general unhappiness, and development of physical symptoms for personal issues (Ambert & Dew, 1982).

Linguistic minority students, particularly recent immigrants, may undergo extreme stress and culture shock and may exhibit, temporarily, signs of behavior disorders. In addition, culturally different students, who may be behaving appropriately for their own cultural groups, may be seen as behaving abnormally in this society's context and may be erroneously labeled as emotionally or behaviorally disordered. On the other hand, linguistic minority students exhibiting extreme signs of emotional disorders may not be identified because their behavior may be explained away in terms of cultural differences.

A third category, that of learning disabled, is defined in P.L. 94-142 as:

> Specific L-D means a disorder in one or more of the basic psychological processes involved in understanding or in using a language, spoken or written, which may manifest itself in an imperfect ability to listen, think, speak, read, write, spell or do math calculations. The term learning disabled does not refer to students who have learning problems which are primarily the result of visual, hearing, or motor handicaps or mentally retarded or culturally, educationally or economically disadvantaged.

In contrast to the federal definition of learning disabilities, Mercer (1973) discovered that in 42 state departments of education, the definition of learning disabilities resulting primarily from environmental "disadvantages" were excluded in only 55% of the regulations. Current definitions, in many state regulations, do not clearly indicate that culturally different children who lack English skills should be excluded from being labeled LD (Gonzales & Ortiz, 1977).

Linguistic minority students who have not reached the level of English necessary to perform cognitive tasks are often misclassified as learning disabled. A misconception exists that if a student has achieved enough language to communicate but is not able to use that language in order to perform more difficult cognitive tasks, then that student must be learning disabled (Cummins, 1976; Duncan & DeAvila, 1979).

According to Cummins (1976) the "threshold level of competence" in each of the child's languages must be determined in order to determine which language should be used to instruct the child. If all other factors are considered equal, the child should be taught in his or her strongest language. Cummins warns against educators demanding that linguistic minority students use English in order to learn when the student has not had the amount of time necessary to develop the level of English language needed to cognitively handle the content. According to Cummins, it takes approximately 5 years for a student to develop a language to a point where he or she can completely function in that language. Therefore, a student asked to perform in a language that he or she has not yet fully developed will perform poorly and can be erroneously classified as LD (Cummins, 1980).

A fifth category comprises communication disorders. When assessing linguistic minority students, the students must be assessed in two languages and findings must be interpreted across language.

Developmental errors made by second language learners in syntax, articulation, and vocabulary are often wrongly labeled as symptomatic of a communication disorder (Ambert & Dew, 1982). The child whose language use should be categorized as different because he or she is developing within the norm and also is acquiring another language or a variety of the same language is often misdiagnosed as having a disorder.

Disorders such as those of hearing and vision and other physical disorders are often undetected in linguistic minority students. For example, according to specialists of the hearing impaired (Fischgrund, 1980), there is a high incidence of hearing loss among Portuguese students that has gone undetected. If linguistic minority students who have physical disorders can be identified, then many of these students can, with minimal remediation, remain in a regular classroom.

A final category which is considered in some states to be included in the definition of exceptional education is giftedness. However, P.L. 94-142 does not consider the gifted child as exceptional.

The most recent definition used is found in Federal Law Section 904 of the Gifted and Talented Children's Act of 1978 which states:

> Gifted and talented children means children who are identified at the preschool, elementary or secondary levels as possessing demonstrated or potential abilities that give evidence of high performance capabilities in areas such as intellectual creative, special academic, or leadership ability, or in performing and visual arts, and who by reason thereof, require services or activities not ordinarily provided by schools.

There are many lists of subjective descriptors thought to define gifted children. The problem is that most linguistic minority students do not gain access to gifted programs because of biased identification procedures, evaluators, and programs lacking bilingual personnel on staff (Ambert & Dew, 1982).

SAFEGUARDING LINGUISTIC MINORITIES IN THE ASSESSMENT PROCESS

It was not until the civil rights movement of the 1960's that the needs of ethnolinguistic groups began to be recognized in this country. Since then, however, there have been legislative, executive, and judicial actions on behalf of ethnic minorities. On the legislative level, Title VI of the Civil Rights Act of 1964 prohibits discrimination on the basis of race, color, or national origin in any federally funded program. Therefore, any school system could be found guilty by the Office of Civil Rights of discriminating against culturally and linguistically different students if that system denies equal access to this population of students. Furthermore, the Bilingual Education Acts (1968, 1974, and 1979), Title IX of the Civil Rights Act (1972), Section 504 of the 1973 Rehabilitation Act, the Equal Education Opportunity Act (1974), and P.L. 94-142 (Education of the Handicapped Act) provide additional legislative protections for linguistically and culturally different students.

On the executive level, the Office of Civil Rights issued both the Federal Lau Remedies (1975) and the well known May 25th O.C.R. Memorandum (1975). The Federal Lau Remedies was the result of the Lau v. Nichols (1974) Supreme Court decision which clearly established the fact that a school cannot claim to provide equal access to limited-English-proficient students by providing them with the same services provided to other children. The decision rendered in the Lau v. Nichols case was on behalf of Chinese students' rights to have support services in their language and in English as a second language. The United States Supreme Court stated that "there is no equality of treatment merely by providing students with the same facilities, textbooks, teachers, and curriculum, for students who do not understand English are effectively foreclosed from any meaningful education." The Lau Remedies demand a transitional bilingual program for all limited-English-proficient students, including those with "disabilities." Specifically, the remedies require that a district implement a systematic procedure for identifying numbers of LEP students in a system, assess the relative language dominance of students in their native language and in English, and provide an appropriate instruction program which would ensure educational opportunity.

The May 25th O.C.R. Memorandum (1975) addressed the issue of inappropriate placement of minority students in special education classes. The memorandum specifically stated that "School districts must not assign national origin, minority group students to classes for the mentally retarded on the basis of criteria which essentially measure or evaluate English language skills."

As a result of the 1970 memorandum, a Task Force was formed by the Director of the Office of Civil Rights. This Task Force consisted of Puerto Rican and Mexican-American educators, social scientists, and community leaders who developed monitoring strategies and recommendations addressing the assessment and placement of minority students in classes for the handicapped (Bergin, 1980).

At the judicial level, the fact that a student's linguistic or cultural difference cannot be used to label a child as "exceptional" or "disabled" has been clearly established in several cases in state courts.

These include: <u>Diana v. The State Board of Education</u> (California, 1973); <u>Larry P. v. Wilson Rites, Superintendent of Public Instruction for the State of California</u> (California, 1979); and <u>Martin Luther King, Jr. Elementary School Children, et al. v. Ann Arbor School District Board</u>, F. Supp. 1371 ED (Michigan, 1979).

In <u>Jose P. et al. v. Gordon M. Ambach et al.</u> (New York, 1979) a New York court mandated that the New York City Board of Education evaluate students in their native language or by whatever means a student is able to communicate.

In <u>Lora v. Board of Education of the City of New York,</u> 465 F. Supp. 1211 (1977), the court asserted that the over-representation of minority students in special education classes violated the rights of minority students.

The <u>Guadalupe v. Tempe Elementary School District</u> case (1971) also raised the issue of the improper use of standardized intelligence tests to place students in classes for the mentally retarded. According to Bergin (1980), an out-of-court settlement of the Guadalupe case provided many of the same provisions agreed to in the Diana case (which involved the misclassification of Mexican Americans in classes for the mentally retarded). In the Guadalupe case, the recognition of disproportionate numbers of Mexican-American and Yaqui Indians in classes for the mentally retarded led to provisions to limit that number systematically, within a limited period of time.

47

The above court decisions have been based on the guaranteed provisions of P.L. 94-142 (The Education for all Handicapped Children Act), which guarantee educational rights for all exceptional children. A most important provision in this act entails that "handicapped" children receive a free appropriate education in the least restrictive environment. Specifically, the provision that a student has the right to be assessed in his or her dominant language and that parents have a right to be communicated with in their home language helps safeguard the rights of linguistic and cultural minorities.

Nevertheless, misclassification and misplacement of linguistic minority students still continues despite P.L. 94-142 safeguards, other legislative mandates, and numerous court cases. According to Bergin (1980), at the time of the Lau Remedies (1975) bilingual teachers began to complain about the rising numbers of exceptional students being placed in bilingual classrooms rather than in special education. The reasons given for this under-representation of linguistic minority exceptional students in special education classes were the inappropriate assessment instruments and the lack of bilingual special education teaching staff and materials. According to Landurand (1981), less than 5% of all limited-English-proficient students enrolled in bilingual programs were evaluated and identified as exceptional. A further research investigation by Nuttall and Landurand (1984) of 20 school districts in the U.S. revealed that a substantially smaller percentage of limited-English-proficient students are being identified for special education than the 12% national incidence figure for special education.

It appears that many linguistic minority students who have inadequate communicative abilities in English are not being identified and referred for special education at a rate equal to their monolingual English-speaking peers. On the other hand, linguistic minority students who have attained some level of English communicative ability are mainstreamed into regular monolingual classes, are disproportionately referred for special education services, and are over-enrolled in special education classes (Landurand, 1981).

Bias in testing has inevitably led to inappropriate placements. Mercer (1973) was the first to document this problem when she found in her Riverside study that the rate of placement for Mexican-American students in classes for the mentally retarded was four times larger than their representation in the total school enrollment. Tucker (1980), studying several school districts in the Southwest, explained the difference in proportions in enrollment as merely a relabeling from mentally retarded to learning disabled.

WHAT IS NONDISCRIMINATORY ASSESSMENT?

"Nondiscriminatory" identification and placement is basically defined by Section 612 (5) (C) 94-142 which says that in order to qualify for assistance, a state must establish appropriate procedures:

Procedures to assure that testing and evaluation materials and procedures utilized for the purpose of evaluation and placement of handicapped children will be selected and administered so as not to be racially or culturally discriminatory. Such materials or procedures shall be provided and administered in the child's native language or mode of communication unless it clearly is not feasible to do so and no single procedure shall be the sole criterion for determining an appropriate educational program for a child.

In determining whether an assessment process is appropriate, the tester, the test, and the testee must all be considered as important components in this dynamic process.

The Tester

Who should test linguistically/culturally different students? All things being equal, a tester who speaks the language of the child, understands the culture of the child, and is a skilled assessor will be the best choice for the child. The examiner's knowledge of the culture of the child, either through birth or training, is also extremely important for understanding the examinee's behavior and perception of the testing situation (Plata, 1982). In addition, Oakland and Matuszek (1977) state that examiners who do not give evidence of a warm, responsive, and receptive but firm style toward minority children will not be able to establish the rapport needed for successful testing and therefore will not obtain the best performance from the child.

Because of the scarcity of native language assessors, many school systems use discriminatory testing practices. Typically, the student is given an evaluation where English language is used as the medium for testing. Because a linguistic minority student may have attained basic oral-aural English skills, it is assumed that this student can be evaluated in English; language proficiency in English and the native language is not determined before testing. Standardized instruments selected by monolingual English psychologists are selected and administered to the student. Scores are computed, even though many psychologists are aware of the irrelevancy of the norms and inappropriateness of many of the items to some children's cultural backgrounds and experience. The result is that little is learned about the child's level of functioning and misclassification is quite likely to occur.

A second common evaluative approach involves a situation where a linguistic minority student, referred for an evaluation, is obviously of limited English proficiency. The school psychologists attempt to evaluate the student with the help of an interpreter. The interpreter is given no training in administering tests. The psychologist is unaware of the accuracy of the interpreted question. The standardized instruments used still contain inappropriate items and still have not been normed on this population. Other potential problems in using interpeters are as follows:

1. The interpreter may not be equally fluent in both languages and may translate incorrectly to the child or to the tester.

2. The interpreter may identify with the child and subconsciously prompt the right responses nonverbally or through other cues.

3. Interpreters are usually not trained or familiar with the principles of test administration, human development, and human relations.

4. Interpreters who are of different social class, race, or ethnic group may be negatively disposed towards the child even though they speak the same language. Because of these and other pitfalls, school systems should either try to avoid using interpreters or to develop special programs to train them (Nuttall & Landurand, 1984).

A third current evaluation practice is to have a limited-English-proficient student evaluated by a bilingual psychologist, who may be unfamiliar with the child's cultural background. Other school personnel, unable to speak the student's language, delegate to the bilingual psychologist total responsibility for evaluating the student and recommending a placement. This practice is risky because the psychologist may be insensitive to the child's cultural background, and/or may also be a poor assessor.

A fourth approach involves a sensitive bilingual psychologist, who understands the limited-English-proficient student and his or her culture and understands how to use evaluation instruments cautiously. The evaluator relies on a multidisciplinary approach to assessment and gathers relevant information about the child from many sources. The results, in this case, will probably be a more accurate assessment of the child's abilities and weaknesses and a more appropriate placement for the child.

The Testee

The child's level of English proficiency, the attitude of the child being tested, and the behavior of the child taking the test all influence the child's performance and the way that performance is interpreted by the tester. The behavior of children during a testing situation is dependent on many factors. The way their culture defines learning, their past experiences with test taking, whether they were reared in a cooperative or competitive environment (Pepitone, 1980), their cognitive style (Castenada & Ramirez, 1974), and their cultural values are all major factors in determining a child's performance on standardized instruments. A child whose culture does not value "time" in the same way as Euro-American middle-class culture will not respond to "timed tests" in the same way as many middle-class Euro-American children. A child who exists in a cooperative learning environment will appear unmotivated in a competitive test-taking environment. In addition, a child who is primarily field-sensitive in his or her relationship to adults and to instructional material will have difficulty responding to a formal situation demanding formal task performance with an impersonal adult. An assessor who understands the cognitive, perceptual, and interactional behaviors of the student can adapt technique and procedures in order to establish the rapport that is necessary for the ethnolinguistic minority student to perform at optimum level.

The Test

The literature on nondiscriminatory assessment has focused primarily on the biases of standardized instruments. Tests have been criticized for "item bias" and improper standardization. Tests used in American schools are generally written by middle-class individuals and reflect an Anglo conformity ideology typical of that class level and culture (Mercer, 1979). Not only do the content items reflect Euro-American middle-class experiences, but values such as competitiveness and emphasis on time also reflect Euro-American middle-class culture. Ethnolinguistic minority students who have not experienced these values and have not learned this content obviously are at a disadvantage in taking these standardized tests.

In addition to item bias, most tests used in the United States are normed on the majority population. Even when tests claim to have included minorities in their standardization population, minorities are included in such small ratios that the results are insignificant in influencing the standardization results.

Furthermore, the interpretation of test scores is of critical importance especially when a culturally or linguistically different student is concerned. The assessor needs to probe further as to the possible reasons for the student's low score. Was the test administered to a limited-English-proficient student in English? Does the student speak a nonstandard dialect and was the test given using a standard native dialect? Was the child unfamiliar with skills needed to take the test? Many questions need to be answered before making any interpretations about the student's performance.

ELIMINATING OR REDUCING BIAS IN TESTING

A widely used approach in testing limited-English-proficient students is to translate and/or adapt standardized tests. This approach implies direct or written translations, weighing the nonverbal portion more heavily than the verbal and varying the speed and power components of the test (Mercer, 1979). The advantages are that this approach is easier than developing new tests. In addition, children's scores improve when given the test in their native languages (Nuttall & Landurand, 1984). Nevertheless, this approach presents many problems. Standardized translated versions of tests do not take into account the many regional dialects spoken by students (Plata, 1982; DeAvila & Havassy, 1974a). In addition, words do not have the same meaning when translated. Words in one language may not have the same frequency of use in a second language (DeAvila & Havassy, 1974b). Therefore, a word that may be considered very basic in a child's second language may be a very difficult or nonexistent word from the perspective of the child's first language. In addition, the content still reflects American middle-class culture (Mercer, 1979; Plata, 1982).

A second approach used is to <u>establish ethnic norms</u>. The intention in developing ethnic norms is to compensate ethnic minority students for their "deprivation." Ethnic norms are problematic in that they have the potential for encouraging lower expectations for minorities. A second problem in this approach is that it does not provide educators with any accurate diagnostic information needed for educational programming. Instead, it may lead to false comparisons between different ethnolinguistic groups. A further problem with establishing ethnic norms is the reinforcement of a false assumption that groups are ethnically homogeneous. Use of ethnic norms will encourage the tendency to assume that lower scores are ultimately indicative of lower potential, thereby contributing to the self-fulfilling prophecy of lower expectations for minorities as well as reinforcing the genetic inferiority argument proposed by Jensen (Jensen & Rosenfeld, 1974) and others.

A third attempt to respond to criticism of standard IQ tests is to <u>create culture-fair tests</u>. Under the category of culture-fair tests are: the common culture approach, the learning potential approach, and the neo-Piagetian approach.

According to Nuttall (Nuttall & Landurand, 1984) the common culture approach employs the use of problems or tasks that are equally familiar or unfamiliar to people in most cultures. These tests tend to be nonverbal, performance oriented, symbolic responses to relationships among figures or designs. The advantages of this approach are that it is economical and can be applied to all groups. Some of these tests minimize dependence on verbal ability (Cervantes, 1974), speed, item content, and test wiseness (Mick, 1982).

This approach has been widely criticized for many reasons. Mercer (1979) and Oakland and Matuszek (1977) contend that this approach is unable to yield similar means and standard deviations for different racial groups and social classes. Mercer (1979) further criticizes this approach for its nonpredictability of academic performance. Mick (1982) points out that several of these tests, for example, the Raven's, require formal skills learned only in a school situation. Oakland and Matuszek (1977) criticize the fact that his approach does not assess important psychological characteristics. Some common tests which fall within the common culture approach are Cattell's Culture Fair Tests for measuring intelligence, Raven's Progressive Matrices (1960), Goodenough Draw-A-Man Test, Leiter International Performance Scale (1966), and Bender-Gestalt Visual Motor Test (1938).

A second approach in the category of developing culture-fair tests is the learning potential approach. In this approach, children are pre- and posttested on a nonverbal reasoning test such as the Ravens. Between tests they are trained to process the test. The difference between the first score and the score after training represents the child's learning potential. Proponents of this approach contend that it gives a measure of the child's ability to learn. Budoff (1976) claims that it predicts nonverbal learning performance in school. Opponents of this approach claim that it is extremely time-consuming, that test data is limited to nonverbal areas, and that it does not predict future academic performance (Mercer, 1979).

An example of the learning potential approach is Raven's Progressive Matrices using a test-train-retest paradigm of Budoff (1974).

A third approach within the category of culture-fair test is the neo-Piagetian approach. This approach consists of applying neo-Piagetian measures to determine cognitive development. According to DeAvila and Havassy (1974b), scores on tests taken in English, Spanish, or bilingually showed no appreciable differences. Performance of Mexican and American samples both were within expected limits of cognitive development for given chronological ages. No ethnic differences were found.

Opponents of this approach cite the following disadvantages: the ability to predict academic performance is unknown, because many school systems do not organize their curricula according to developmental states; the practical uses of this test are limited; and Piagetian cognitive theory is difficult for teachers and parents to understand.

Examples of this approach (Nuttall & Landurand, 1984) are the Piagetian measure developed by DeAvila and Struthers, including Cartoon Conservation Scales. Measures are computerized to give information and recommendation to parents, teachers, and administrators through a system called PAPI (Program Assessment Pupil Interaction) (DeAvila & Havassy, 1974a).

A fourth approach to diminish discrimination in assessment is the creation of culture-specific tests. These are specific tests designed for each major American microcultural group (Laosa, 1977). The advantage of this approach is that it allows the child to be assessed at his or her level of functioning relative to expectations of his or her family and subculture (Mercer, 1979). This approach further highlights the fact that test performance is highly dependent upon the degree to which the test reflects the test taker's own culture. There are several criticisms of this approach. It is impossible to construct tests for every microculture. In addition, a student's performance on these tests does not predict the child's ability to function in relation to American core culture (Mercer, 1979). Examples of culture-specific tests are: Black Intelligence Test of Cultural Homogeneity (BITCH-100). This test includes 100 multiple choice vocabulary items which deal exclusively with Black culture. However, since the vocabulary list was chosen from the dictionary of American slang, it is probably biased against middle-class Blacks.

A second test, the Enchilada Test, contains 31 multiple choice items which deal with Mexican-American barrio life. These tests, which are designed for a specific ethnic microcultural group, may not be appropriate for use with those individuals who may be acculturated into the dominant society.

A fifth approach is Mercer's multipluralistic approach. This approach uses parent interview and student testing in comprehensive assessment of the whole child (including medical, sociocultural, intellectual, and behavioral aspects). This approach develops multiple normative frameworks for sociocultural, socioeconomic, racial-ethnic, and geographic groups. A student's estimated learning potential is computed by comparing his or her score with the average score for persons from similar backgrounds.

The SOMPA (System of Multi Pluralistic Assessment) has advantages and disadvantages. It provides comprehensive information to classify a child. Another claimed advantage is that it is easier to renorm existing tests and obtain information from parents than to develop new unbiased tests (Nuttall, 1979). However, SOMPA has been heavily criticized. Some major criticisms include the following: the validity of the SOMPA is just beginning to be established (Nuttall, 1979); lack of national norms is a major drawback (Nuttall, 1979); the length of the battery makes it impractical for routine use (Plata, 1982); the estimated learning potential does not predict achievement (Oakland & Matuszek, 1977). Because the estimated learning potential is designed to predict how well a student could perform in an optimum socioculturally pluralistic learning environment, and because very few of those environments actually exist, the estimated learning potential becomes educationally useless for purposes of educational planning and programming. An additional two criticisms of the SOMPA are that some minorities find the "regression formula" concept demeaning. The process of adding points to a student's score because of the student's sociocultural background is viewed by some minorities as more harmful than helpful. In addition, SOMPA does not provide useful diagnostic information to program for the child.

A sixth approach is a task analysis approach. In this approach the tester analyzes the skills and behavior required to answer each test item and determines why the child does not respond correctly. The child is then trained in the areas of weakness and retested (Kaufman, 1977). Because emphasis is on the mastery of content, the advantage of this approach is that children are treated as individuals and not compared to others. In addition, treatment is an integral part of the task analysis model. The model is essentially a test-teach-test approach (Mercer & Ysseldyke, 1977). A criticism of this approach is that some of the methods of analyzing the tasks can become difficult as tasks become complex (Kaufman, 1977). Another criticism is that this approach has been used mostly in academic achievement areas. Examples of this approach are the Key Math Test and the Woodcock Reading Mastery Test. According to Nuttall et al. (1983), exponents include Kaufman (1977), Resnick, Wang, and Kaplan (1973), Gold (1972), and Bijou (1970).

A seventh approach is <u>criterion-referenced tests</u>. Unlike norm-referenced tests, criterion-referenced measures are used to compare an individual with established criteria or performance standards, and not with other individuals (Popham & Husek, 1969). A strength in this method is that it evaluates a child on clearly specified educational tasks (Mowder, 1980) and is directly interpretable in terms of specific standards (Oakland & Matuszek, 1977). There are several cited disadvantages to this approach; for example, reliability and validity are difficult to ascertain and cultural biases are hard to eliminate (Oakland & Matuszek, 1977).

A second criticism is that selecting appropriate behavioral objectives and criteria can prove to be both difficult and time consuming (Laosa, 1977).

A third criticism is that the tendency to use these tests to establish standards of excellence or desirable educational goals should be avoided (Oakland & Matuszek, 1977). An example of this approach is SOBER-Espanol, which provides comprehensive evaluation for Spanish reading (Nuttall, 1979).

An eighth and final approach is the <u>global approach to test bias</u>. In this approach, nonbiased assessment is viewed as a process rather than a set of instruments. Multifactored assessment values language dominance, adaptive behavior, and sociocultural background (Reschly, 1978). Every step in the assessment process is evaluated as a possible source of bias (Tucker, 1980). The advantage of this approach is that it is the most comprehensive and realistic approach so far developed to aid the practitioner in identifying the sources of bias operating in the assessment system. The disadvantages in this approach are that it underestimates the role of content bias of tests, it is too time consuming and it does not guarantee eliminating bias. Examples of this approach include the <u>Guide for Non-biased Assessment</u> (NRRC, 1976) and Tucker's (1980) <u>Nineteen Steps for Assuring Non-biased Placement of Students in Special Education</u>.

Based on the author's experience with local school assessment procedures in relation to limited-English-proficient students, the global approach to assessment is highly preferred as a necessary first step in assessing any student. Other approaches, such as criterion-referenced, task-analysis, and test-train-retest models need to be pursued, particularly with the LEP population.

COMMON ASSESSMENT PRACTICES

Several surveys (Bogatz, 1978; Coulopolous & De George, 1982; Mick, 1982; Morris, 1977) have described the testing practices used by school personnel to assess limited-English-proficient children.

In a 1977 survey of 12 large school systems (in Arizona, California, Colorado, Florida, Illinois, Nevada, and Texas), Morris found that the four tests most commonly used were the Bender-Gestalt Test, Draw-A-Person, Leiter International Performance Scale, and Wechsler Intelligence Scale for Children (WISC-English version). The first three of these tests fit in the common culture approach to diminishing bias because they involve less reliance on verbal skills than some other approaches.

According to Nuttall et al. (1983), 5 years later when Coulopolous and De George surveyed 21 school psychologists in Massachusetts, they found that the four most frequently used tests were the same ones obtained by Morris, even though other instruments and approaches were available. The study found that English-speaking psychologists administered the tests using interpreters, pantomime, or whatever amount of English the child had mastered.

In the largest study of all, Mick (1982) surveyed 157 administrators of special education in four states (Texas, New Mexico, Florida, and Massachusetts) and two cities (Philadelphia and New York). She reported her results in terms of assessment "modifications" for bilingual (Hispanic) students rather then in terms of specific tests used. However, Mick reported that nonverbal subscales were frequently used. Criterion-referenced tests, pluralistic assessments, and culture-fair tests were used only occasionally. The most frequent modification cited was the use of language proficiency tests. Modifications used only occasionally included matching the examiner to the examinee, observing the child in the classroom, and using interpreters. Testers seldom attempted to improve the child's test-taking skills or to use local ethnic norms (Nuttall, 1983).

In the 21 school systems surveyed in the Nuttall and Landurand report (1984) to the Office of Bilingual Education and Minority Language Affairs (OBEMLA), the most frequently used testing approaches were the common-culture approach and adaptations/translations of existing tests. None of the systems reported using the culture-specific approach or the global approach. Seven of the 21 systems reported using the multipluralistic approach in total or in selected parts, mainly the adaptive battery (ABTC).

ARE THERE VIABLE ALTERNATIVE COMPREHENSIVE CROSS-CULTURAL APPROACHES?

After reviewing the research in the assessment of linguistically culturally different students, this author contends that of the approaches presented, the global approach to test bias offers the most promise because of its emphasis on the process of evaluation. In addition, for each child from a linguistic minority background, a multidisciplinary assessment team should be composed. This team should include at least one person who speaks the child's language and is familiar with the child's culture and one person experienced in bilingual education, preferably in the child's language.

Prior to conducting any assessments, a determination of the child's level of proficiency in both the native language and in English must be made. Care should be taken in selecting instruments that claim to test proficiency. Both oral and written proficiency must be determined. In cases where there are no instruments to test proficiency in a child's native language, an informal assessment approach needs to be developed to make this information available.

The child should be observed by the assessment team in a variety of settings, including the classroom. The child's functioning in each of these settings should be described.

A team member thoroughly knowledgeable about the child's culture and language should prepare a home survey after visiting the child in the home setting. This team member should ascertain not only the child's educational background, but what language(s) the family normally speaks, what language(s) is spoken in the neighborhood, and what exposure the child has had to the English-speaking core culture. Information about the child's previous history and experience is critical in cross-cultural assessment.

A medical examination is an important aspect of cross-cultural assessment. Often, linguistically and culturally different students are placed in restrictive special education settings when their problem(s) could easily have been corrected by eyeglasses, hearing aids, or other physical devices. Many physical problems which can be easily rectified go undetected because the child does not receive a medical examination.

A fourth area of assessment which is often overlooked when working with linguistic minority students is the educational assessment component. At minimum, reading and math diagnostic assessments must be conducted in both the native language and English. It is not enough to know that a 10-year-old child is performing in English at a second-grade level. What specific skills does the child display in both languages? In which specific areas does the child display skills in one language? In which specific areas does the child display a lack of skills in both languages?

Instruments such as Key Math Diagnostic and Woodcock-Johnson may be helpful in determining the child's academic achievement status. Informal reading and math inventories in the native languages of LEP students must be developed. This requires native-language speakers, preferably those who understand the child's educational background, and skilled educational diagnosticians.

All assessments should focus on determining how the child functions both socially and cognitively in both English and the native language. Therefore, all procedures and techniques should be administered by an appropriately qualified professional who is familiar with the child's culture and who speaks the child's language. If, after every attempt has been made, there is no appropriately qualified professional to conduct these assessments, then an interpreter needs to be sought and trained to work skillfully with the monolingual assessor. Cross-training and teaming needs to occur between interpreter and monolingual assessor.

RECOMMENDATIONS

The area of providing appropriate assessment for children from linguistic minorities is plagued by a general lack of information. Many local districts and states do not presently collect data on these children. Data should be collected on numbers of children in particular language groups in various monolingual regular, bilingual, and special education programs. Available data should be collected on the number of children from linguistic minorities who have limited communication skills in English, according to language group. Specific information is needed on linguistic minorities who have educational handicapping conditions according to category of handicap, type of placement, and language group. Of this group of linguistic minorities, a breakdown of limited-English-proficient students by handicap and placement is needed. It is very important that the Office of Education require that states request this information from local districts. Information of this nature should be coordinated, interpreted, and disseminated.

The development of an effective system to collect, analyze, and disseminate data about linguistic minority children is an important first step toward a better understanding of the problem (Nuttall & Landurand, 1984, p. 11).

Considering the high risk of inappropriate educational placements for linguistic minority children, it is critical that bilingual and special education programs work closely together. In many states, bilingual special education programs are nonexistent or not defined clearly. There is an overall lack of coordination at federal, state, and local levels. Because of this lack of coordination, inappropriate assessment procedures and placements continue to occur. Staff should be assigned at the local and state level to coordinate and monitor assessment, placement, and programming of linguistic minority students. Once this coordination is in place, then areas such as developing standards for assessors in competency in the language and guidelines for use of interpreters in assessment of limited-English-proficient children can be addressed.

A third area of critical need is the scarcity of training personnel. A major need cited by bilingual and special education directors in 20 states is for bilingual certified assessors and specialists to serve linguistic minority exceptional students. Many states have no guidelines for determining many levels of linguistic competency for those professionals assessing children from linguistic minority groups.

A third recommendation is that the Office of Education assume a leadership position in addressing training needs in bilingual special education. The Office of Special Education should require that state agencies, in their comprehensive system of personnel development, address the issue of staff development in bilingual special education. Funds should be appropriated in this area. The development of a cadre of trained personnel must be addressed.

Research in this area is needed in order to determine the best methods of assessing the targeted children. The effect of a child's cognitive style on performance is one area among many that needs further research. The Office of Education should, through requests for proposals, encourage needed research in the area of cross-cultural assessment.

As stated throughout this paper, current assessment practices result in inappropriate placements for children of minority ethnolinguistic backgrounds. At present, assessment of children from linguistic minorities is often conducted in English, if the child understands the language at all. If not, assessments are conducted through an interpreter, who may have little if any knowledge of assessment. The reliance on inappropriate instruments continues. A comprehensive system of assessment for ethnolinguistic children should be developed. This system should encompass at the state level a development of policies and a means of monitoring the implementation of these guidelines at the local level.

Cross-cultural assessment is an area plagued with problems, problems stemming from lack of administrative coordination, lack of trained personnel who speak minority languages, lack of descriptive data, lack of clearly articulated guidelines and procedures, and lack of research. If linguistic minority students are to receive appropriate assessments, placements, and programs, emphasis must be placed on addressing the above areas and not on finding the appropriate tests. There will never be a test or tests constructed to solve all the problem(s) in cross-cultural assessment. The minority ethnolinguistic child needs to be understood and described in his or her cultural and linguistic context at home, in the community, and at school. A well-articulated, creative, comprehensive cross-cultural approach is needed in order to do this. Can we meet this need--this challenge?

REFERENCES

Advisory Board of Access. (March 1981). <u>National task-oriented seminar</u> <u>in bilingual special education personnel preparation</u>. Unpublished paper.

Ambert, A., & Dew, N. (1982). <u>Special education for exceptional bilingual</u> <u>students: A handbook for educators</u>. University of Wisconsin-Milwaukee, Midwest National Origin Desegregation Assistance Center.

Bergin, Victoria. (1980). <u>Special education needs in bilingual programs</u>. Inter America Research Associates, Inc., National Clearinghouse for Bilingual Education.

Bogatz, B.E. (1978). <u>With bias toward none</u>. Coordinating Office of Regional Resource Centers, University of Kentucky.

Budoff, M. (June 1974). <u>Measuring learning potential: An alternative</u> <u>to the traditional psychological examination</u>. Paper presented at the First Annual Study Conference in School Psychology, Temple University, Philadelphia.

Castenada, A., & Ramirez, M. (1974). <u>Cultural democracy, bi-cognitive</u> <u>development and education</u>. Academic Press.

Cervantes, R. A. (April 1974). <u>Problems and alternatives in testing</u> <u>Mexican American students</u>. ERIC Document. Paper presented at annual meeting of the American Educational Research Association, Chicago Il.

Cole, N. S. (1981). Bias in testing, <u>American Psychologist</u>, <u>36</u>(10), 1067-1077.

Coulopoulos, D., & De George, G. (1982). <u>Current methods and practices</u> <u>of school psychologists in the assessment of linguistic minority</u> <u>children</u>. Massachusetts Department of Education, Division of Special Education.

Cummins, J. (1976). The influence of bilingualism on cognitive growth: A synthesis of research findings and explanatory hypothesis. <u>Working</u> <u>Papers on Bilingualism</u>, <u>9</u>, 1-43.

Cummins, J. (1979). Cognitive/Academic language proficiency, linguistic interdependence, the optimal age question and some other matters. <u>Working Papers on Bilingualism</u>, <u>19</u>.

Cummins, J. (1980). The entry and exit fallacy in bilingual education. <u>NABE Journal</u> <u>4</u>, 25-29.

Cummins, J. (1981). The role of language development in promoting educational success for language minority students. In <u>Schooling</u> <u>and language minority students, a theoretical framework</u>, pp. 3-49. Los Angeles: Evaluating Dissemination and Assessment Center.

DeAvila, E., & Havassy, B. (1974a). Piagetian alternative to I.Q.: Mexican-American Study. In N. Hobbs (Ed.), <u>Issues in the classification of exceptional children</u>. San Francisco: Jossey-Bass.

DeAvila, E., & Havassy, B. (1974b). The testing of minority children-A neo-Piagetian approach. <u>Today's Education</u>, November-December.

Duncan, S. E., & DeAvila, E. A. (1979). Bilingualism and cognition: Some recent findings. <u>NABE Journal</u>, <u>4</u>, 15-50.

Fischgrund, Joseph. (1980). Personal interview.

Gonzalez, G. (1974). Language, culture, and exceptional children. <u>Exceptional Children</u>, <u>40</u>, 565-570.

Gonzalez, G., & Ortiz, L. (1977). Social policy and education related to linguistically and culturally different groups. <u>Journal of Learning Disabilities</u>.

Grossman, H. J. (Ed.). (1977). <u>Manual on terminology and classification in mental retardation</u>. Washington DC: American Association on Mental Deficiency.

Jensen, M., & Rosenfeld, L. B. (1974). Influence of mode of presentation, ethnicity, and social class on teachers' evaluations of students. <u>Journal of Educational Psychology</u>, <u>66</u>, 540-547.

Kaufman, J. (1977). <u>Proceedings of a multicultural colloquium on non-biased pupil assessment</u>. Bureau of School Psychological and Social Services, New York State Department of Education.

Landurand, P. (1977). <u>Bisep Report</u>. Quincy: Massachusetts Department of Education, Division of Special Education.

Landurand, P. (1981, February). <u>Culturally responsive education: Where are we, where are we going, and how do we get there?</u> Paper presented at The Council for Exceptional Children Conference on the Exceptional Bilingual Child, New Orleans.

Laosa, L. M. (1977). Nonbiased assessment of children's abilities: Historical antecedents and current issues. In T. Oakland (Ed.), <u>Psychological and educational assessment of minority children</u>. New York: Brunner/Mazel.

Mercer, J. (1973). <u>Labeling the mentally retarded: Clinical and social systems perspectives on mental retardation</u>. Berkeley CA: University of California Press.

Mercer, J. R. (1979). <u>SOMPA: System of Multicultural Pluralistic Assessment</u>. <u>Technical manual</u>. New York: Psychological Corporation.

Mercer, J. R., & Ysseldyke, J. (1977). Designing diagnostic-intervention programs. In T. Oakland (Ed.), <u>Psychological and educational assessment of minority children</u>. New York: Brunner/Mazel.

Mick, D. B. (1982). <u>Assessment procedures and enrollment patterns of Hispanic students in special education and gifted programs</u>. Unpublished doctoral dissertation, Ohio State University.

Morris, J. (1977). What tests do schools use with Spanish-speaking students? <u>Integrated Education</u>, <u>15</u>(2), 21-37.

Mowder, B. (1980). A strategy for the assessment of bilingual handicapped children. <u>Psychology in the schools</u>, <u>17</u>(1).

Nuttall, E. V. (1979). Test reviews: System of multipluralistic assessment. <u>Journal of Educational Measurement</u>, <u>16</u>(4).

Nuttall, E. V., & Landurand, P. (1984). <u>A study of mainstreamed limited English proficient handicapped students in bilingual education</u>. Wayland MA: Vazquez-Nuttall, Inc.

Oakland, T. & Matuszek, P. (1977). Using tests in nondiscriminatory assessment. In T. Oakland (Ed.), <u>Psychological and educational assessment of minority children</u>, New York: Brunner/Mazel.

Olmedo, E. L. (1981). Testing linguistic minorities. <u>American Psychologist</u>, <u>36</u>(10), 1078-1085.

Pepitone, E. (1980). <u>Children in cooperation and competition</u>. Lexington MA: D.C. Heath.

Plata, M. (1982). <u>Assessment, placement, and programming of bilingual exceptional pupils: A practical approach</u>. Reston VA: The Council for Exceptional Children.

Popham, W. J., & Husek, T. R. (1969). Implications of criterion-referenced measurement. <u>Journal of Educational Measurement</u>, <u>6</u>, 1-9.

Reschly, D. J. (1978). WISC-R factor structures among Anglos, Blacks, Chicanos, and native-American Papagos. <u>Journal of Consulting and Clinical Psychology</u>, <u>46</u>(3), 417-422.

Tucker, J. A. (1980). <u>Nineteen steps for assuring nonbiased placement of students in special education</u>. Reston VA: The Council for Exceptional Children.

CHAPTER 3

COGNITIVE DEVELOPMENT AND LEARNING IN MILDLY HANDICAPPED BILINGUAL CHILDREN

Robert Rueda

According to a recent American Association on Mental Deficiency (AAMD) presentation (Levine & Langness, 1983), psychologists are beginning to look at behavior, especially language and cognition, as it occurs in everyday life. As Levine points out, there are at least two reasons to do so:

1. The issue of ecological validity, i.e., do cognitive tasks in the laboratory represent real life?

2. The converse of the above: namely, to try to produce instances of cognition and problem solving which might be adapted for more controlled laboratory studies.

As a result of this more intense focus on behavior in natural contexts, there has been much discussion regarding the relative merits of both the methods and theoretical bases for experimental, laboratory-based research as opposed to research taking place in everyday settings (see, for example, Brooks & Baumeister, 1977). This has been loosely called the distinction between quantitative and qualitative approaches. (See, for example, Edgerton & Langness, 1978, and Price-Williams & Gallimore, 1980 for more extended discussions of this issue.) Although this issue continues to generate much controversy, it seems reasonable to assume that these different perspectives both answer important questions, and that neither need be excluded from the researcher's "bag of tricks." Rather, the use of a particular paradigm should be fitted to the question being asked. The need for a variety of theoretical and methodological approaches is evident when considering the complex developmental and educational issues raised by looking at special education children who speak or are exposed to more than one language. Therefore, the current collaborative work of several colleagues and me, on special education children exposed to more than one language, incorporates a variety of perspectives.

In this paper, I will briefly describe two lines of ongoing work in the general area of cognition and cognitive development in mildly handicapped children who are bilingual. One focus of this work in this general area has been the question of how access to two languages affects cognitive development. The first section of this paper, therefore, examines the theoretical background and empirical studies concerned with the relationship between language and cognition in bilingual children and bilingual mildly retarded children.

The second section, based upon work currently in progress, concerns an examination of cognitive and interactional factors in the acquisition of literacy. This section is based on an ongoing microethnographic, qualitative look at literacy development and social interaction in a special education classroom with bilingual children (Rueda & Flores, 1984). In this section, a case will be made for the consideration of learning as an interactive process, and for a move away from views of learning as primarily a "within-child" phenomenon.

LANGUAGE AND COGNITION IN BILINGUAL RETARDED CHILDREN

A recent article by Diaz (1983) outlined four widely held beliefs regarding the effects of bilingual education:

1. Children who are instructed bilingually from an early age will suffer cognitive or intellectual retardation in comparison with their monolingually instructed counterparts.

2. They will not achieve the same level of content mastery as their monolingually instructed counterparts.

3. They will not achieve acceptable native language or target language skills.

4. The majority will become anomic individuals without affiliation to either ethnolinguistic group.

Although there is little or no existing evidence, it is commonly assumed that the above mentioned negative effects on cognitive development due to bilingualism should be even more harmful to special education children than to those without special learning problems. Although little empirical work has been carried out on this question with special education children, a significant amount of research has been done with bilingual children without learning problems. A detailed report of this literature is beyond the scope of this paper; however, recent reviews by Diaz (1983) and Rueda (1983) summarize the work which has been done to date on this topic.

In general, the early work on the relationship between bilingualism and intellectual functioning suggested negative outcomes on a variety of dependent measures (Brown, Fournier, & Moyer, 1977; Darcy, 1963; Jensen, 1962, Peal & Lambert, 1962; Yela, 1975). The majority of early studies has been criticized for methodological errors, especially selection bias, instrumentation bias, and lack of control for language proficiency.

In contrast to this early work, later studies have supported a modification of these conclusions. Several investigations have found positive advantages in favor of bilinguals in certain cognitive domains. These have included concept formation (Peal & Lambert, 1962); mental flexibility (Leopold, 1939-49); reasoning and divergent thinking (Cummins & Gulutsan, 1974); separating word-sound and word-meaning (Ianco-Worrall, 1972; Ben Zeev, 1972); the abilities to manipulate and understand language as an abstract tool (Feldman & Shen, 1971; Cummins, 1978); and Piagetian reasoning skills (Liedtke & Nelson, 1968; Feldman & Shen, 1971; Kessler & Quinn 1979; Duncan & DeAvila, 1979).

Theoretical Frameworks

The work of Cummins (1978) has been used extensively as a theoretical framework in the interpretation of the numerous and sometimes conflicting studies dealing with language and cognitive development in bilinguals Specifically, it appears that there exists some theoretical threshold level of language proficiency necessary for the positive effects of bilingualism to be manifested. Further, there appears to be a second minimal threshold of language proficiency below which negative effects on cognitive development might be hypothesized.

A second theoretical framework for examining the effects of bilingualism on cognitive development is based upon a more Piagetian model (DeAvila & Duncan, 1981; DeAvila & Pulos, 1979; Kessler & Quinn, 1979). This may seem strange given the Piagetian emphasis that language follows cognitive development and that the acquisition of more than one language should have no particular consequences for a child's cognitive development. However, some researchers have argued that bilingualism represents an enriched form of experience that could potentially positively influence cognition (DeAvila & Duncan, 1981; Kessler & Quinn, 1979).

DeAvila and Duncan (1981) have discussed the notion of conceptual disequilibrium, a key element in the Piagetian developmental framework, as leading to the integration of schemes within the bilingual child's repertoire. This, in turn, is seen as the basis for cognitive development. As DeAvila and Duncan state, "...it is this capacity to integrate schemes to produce novel acts that defines intelligence or capacity" (p. 341). This process has been closely linked to the notions of metacognition and metalinguistic awareness by DeAvila and Duncan (1981) in their presentation and discussion of a "Metaset" theory of cognitive development of bilinguals based upon a Piagetian framework. An additional part of this theoretical framework proposes generalization of positive cognitive effects to other areas of cognition as well.

Bilingualism and Cognition in Mildly Retarded Children

As has been discussed, current theory proposes that proficient bilinguals might be expected to have a head start in certain cognitive areas such as an understanding of the arbitrary uses of language, cognitive flexibility, etc. As DeAvila and Duncan (1981) suggest, this is a key aspect of metacognition. Mentally retarded children who are also bilingual represent a theoretically interesting group for study with regard to this last point. For example, one area of particular difficulty in terms of cognitive functioning for mentally retarded individuals is in the appropriate use of strategic behavior. This difficulty in the use of strategic behavior has been closely linked with metacognitive awareness and skills (Campione & Brown, 1977).

In essence, the preceding discussion results in a contradiction in terms. That is, by virtue of the deficits associated with mental retardation, children with this label might be expected to exhibit problems in metacognitive awareness and strategic behavior in general. However, by virtue of being bilingual, such children might be expected to be more advanced in the very same or related cognitive domains. Although there is little empirical work available, previous research with nonhandicapped children suggests that bilingual mildly retarded children might exhibit improved cognitive functioning with respect to a matched group of monolinguals.

The above hypothesis was tested in a recent study in which the cognitive performance of mildly retarded chldren with moderate levels of language proficiency in Spanish and English was compared with that of a matched group of monolingual children (Rueda, 1983). In that study, 23 mildly retarded subjects between the ages of 10 and 12 and with WISC IQ scores in the range of to 50-70 were compared with a matched group of monolingual subjects. The language proficiency of the bilingual subjects was assessed beforehand through the use of the Language Assessment Scales, and only bilingual subjects who scored at level three in both of their languages were included in the study. (Although this is not considered "proficient," it does reflect the delayed language skills of retarded children. Further, more stringent criteria for inclusion of bilinguals would have reduced the sample size to an unworkable number.)

The cognitive measures used in the study included a Piagetian measure as well as three metalinguistic measures borrowed from Osherson and Markham (1975) and Cummins (1978). In spite of the limitations of the study (small sample sizes, only moderate proficiency on the part of the bilingual subjects, and failure to measure the language skills of the monolingual sample), it was found that the bilingual group did not differ from the monolingual group on the Piagetian measure, and, therefore, did not suffer any harmful effects as a result of exposure to two languages. Further, there were differences in favor of the bilingual group in some items of the metalinguistic tasks.

A follow-up investigation (Whitaker, Rueda, & Prieto, 1984) examined in more detail a further aspect of DeAvila and Duncan's (1981) Metaset theory. Specifically, the question of interest concerned the suggestion regarding the generalization of bilingual advantages to areas of cognition other than Piagetian and metalinguistic skills. This was examined in a study similar to the previous investigation by incorporating as a dependent measure information processing tasks which have not been previously used in those studies finding cognitive advantages for bilingual students.

The subjects in this investigation included 45 mildly retarded children between 7 and 8 years old. Subjects were selected and classified into three equal groups, including a low language proficient group, a high language proficient group, and a monolingual group based upon scores on the Language Assessment Scales. The cognitive dependent measures consisted of two neo-Piagetian tasks (the Cartoon Conservation Scales and a Static Imagery Task) and an information processing task (A Circular Recall Task). The Static Imagery Task (Inhelder & Piaget, 1971) incorporates two subtasks, a recognitory memory task and a reconstruction memory task. These subtasks involve copying an array of geometric forms from memory after having been presented a model, and then indicating whether various geometric forms had been part of the original array. The Circular Recall Task consists of the ordered recall of a serially presented list of items that are seen only once, with recall to begin on the last few items and end on the first few items (Belmont, Ferretti, & Mitchell, 1982). A 3/4 circular recall task was used in this study, in which recall begins with the last three items and ends with the first four items.

In summary, the high linguistic proficient bilinguals outperformed the low proficient bilinguals and the monolingual subjects on the dependent measures. In addition, there were moderate but signifiant correlations between the dependent measures.

Summary

The results of the last two studies are consistent with previous research which suggest that proficient bilinguals will demonstrate advantages in certain cognitive domains (Duncan and DeAvila, 1979; Cummins, 1978). The results of these studies suggest that the effects of bilingualism (given a relatively high degree of proficiency) are not detrimental to mildly handicapped children and that the same cognitive advantages which accrue to proficient bilinguals will also be evident in bilinguals who are mentally retarded. However, in light of the outcomes of the low linguistic proficient group, it appears that possible linguistic thresholds may exist for handicapped as well for nonhandicapped children.

Although present research suggests cognitive advantages for proficient bilingual mildly retarded children, there are no information processing studies with this group of children (Diaz, 1983). It has not clearly and empirically been demonstrated what cognitive processes (as opposed to products, or test scores) differentiate bilingual from monolingual children when anomalous cognitive development is present. Therefore, future research on the relationship between language and cognition in bilinguals should begin to specify the actual differences in processes between bilingual and monolingual mentally retarded children.

In the following section, work of a more qualitative nature will be summarized. Of particular importance in this next section is the difference in the theoretical perspective and the implications for conceptualizing cognitive activities, including learning.

PERSPECTIVES ON COGNITIVE DEVELOPMENT AND LEARNING:
INTERACTIONAL FRAMEWORK

Although research on social interactional processes and on cognition are conceptualized as unrelated areas of investigation, there is increasing evidence that cognitive outcomes and social interactional processes are intimately related (Mehan, 1978). One cognitive area where this persepctive has been usefully exploited is in research on the acquisition and use of literacy (LCHC Newsletter, 1983; Rueda & Mehan, 1984). This is a topic of great importance with relation to special education children, since problems in the acquisition and use of literacy are formidable for these children. In the following discussion, research on literacy from an interactional framework will be briefly summarized, as well as the underlying theoretical framework guiding the research. This will be used to argue for a reconceptualization of learning as an interactive activity in contrast to a common view of learning as an outcome determined only by child characteristics.

This discussion and summary of ongoing work builds on an earlier research project originating at the Laboratory of Comparative Human Cognition at the University of California at San Diego, concerning school-related learning disabilities, especially in the area of reading (LCHC Newsletter, 1982; Cole and Griffin, 1983). One important outcome of that work was the realization that the children in the project were poor readers at least in part because their conceptualization of reading was basically incorrect. That is, rather than viewing reading as an integrated, whole activity which allows one to gain useful information about the world, they viewed reading as reading out loud for teacher approval. Part of this problem, at least, can be traced back to the decontextualized, "discrete-step" fashion which characterizes most instruction (see LCHC Newsletter, 1982, for further discussion of this issue). In our current work on writing, it has become evident that there is a great deal of overlap in the issues involved, both at the theoretical and applied levels of analysis. In order to provide a context for this work, a brief description of the guiding theoretical frameworks will be presented.

Theoretical Background

The research on literacy previously referred to has been guided by two seemingly different theoretical approaches that in actuality are complementary because they are both based upon the study of _learning as interaction_ (learning in this sense includes the development of literacy over a period of time). This is a critical point, in light of the usual conceptualization of "cognitive style" and "learning style" as uniquely within-child characteristics. That is, learning activities and outcomes are assumed to depend entirely on cognitive and learning attributes that the child brings to the learning encounter. In the frameworks to be presented, the unit of analysis is shifted to the _activity_ and the accompanying interaction (of which the child is only a part), instead of focusing exclusively on the child.

The first approach is the microethnographic approach to the study of schooling, and the second is the sociohistorical approach to the study of learning and development. Each will be described briefly in turn.

A basic premise of microethnographic studies is that social events such as classroom lessons and activities are interactional accomplishments (McDermott, 1977). Hence, a primary goal of such studies is to characterize the structures of lessons or other educational events by describing the interactional work of the participants that assemble their structures (Au, 1980; Mehan, 1979; Schultz, Florio, & Erickson, 1980).

A second theoretical base for this work is drawn from a body of research developed by the Soviet investigators of the sociohistorical school (e.g., Vygotsky, 1978; Wertsch, 1981). This framework has been used and expanded upon here in the United States, especially regarding the relationship between culturally organized experiences and learning (Brown & French, 1979; LCHC, 1982). These ideas are particularly useful because they emphasize how interactions between people become the principal mechanism by which learning and development occurs. In the study of any learning activity, the unit of analysis becomes the act or system of acts by which learning is composed. For example, a critical task in the analysis of writing becomes the careful and detailed description of the learning activity and its constituent sequence of acts including the interactional context in which it is embedded. These sequences of acts are jointly produced or collaboratively assembled by the student and others in his environment.

Another key part of the sociohistorical approach is that the intellectual skills acquired by children are considered to be directly related to how they interact with adults and peers in specific problem-solving environments. That is, children internalize the kind of help they receive from more capable other and eventually come to use the means of guidance initially provided by another to direct their own subsequent problem-solving behaviors. As can be seen, an explicit and direct connection is made between interactions between people and individual psychological processes. The path by which activities are moved from the level of social experience to that of individual experience (see Vygotsky, 1978) consists of a series of transformations. These transformations are the result of a number of developmental events. These events occur in learning situations which Vygotsky called the "zone of proximal development." This is defined as:

> ...the distance between the actual developmental level as determined by independent problem solving and the level of potential development as determined through problem solving under adult guidance or in collaboration with more capable peers. (1978, p. 86)

Within this framework, the student's entering skills are perceived as a major determinant of the starting point of the zone. The kinds of skills that the teachers, schools, parents, and others want the child to master define the farthest end point of the zone. Implicit in this notion is that learning must precede development. This means that teaching oriented toward developmental levels that have already been reached is likely to be ineffective. Good teaching is that which provides students with goal-directed, meaningful, learning experiences which are in advance of development, thus guiding and creating its future. The activities which are organized in the classroom and engaged in by children provide the necessary practice to move the child from the initial, aided level to the final, independent level. It is exactly these activites, in the domain of writing, which have been the focus of attention in ongoing classroom observations.

In the work to be described here, preliminary observations of an ongoing investigation into bilingual mildly handicapped childrens' literacy development in a self-contained classroom have begun to be analyzed. In this investigation, naturalistic field methodology has been used extensively to examine the frequency, types, and processes of social construction involved in literacy events, especially those involving writing. In the present research, by examining literacy events, an attempt has been made to take into account that literacy is an interactional activity. Given this assumption, an effort has been made to specify the ways in which writing activities and events are constructed in both traditional drill-type, decontextualized writing activities as well as in more communicative-based, "authentic" writing activities.

Although the entire scope of the project has encompassed a number of issues including language use by the bilingual students and the accompanying participant structures (Phillips, 1972), the comments here will focus on a brief description of writing in the classroom under observation.

Classroom Description

The classroom in which we have conducted our observations is a self-contained, cross-categorical (learning disabled, emotionally handicapped, and educable mentally handicapped) secondary setting (e.g., grades 4-6). Eight of the students are labeled as learning disabled, one is labeled mentally handicapped, and four are labeled emotionally handicapped.

Writing Activities in the Classroom

This classroom has been of particular interest because of the approach to reading and writing embodied by the teacher. Briefly, the teacher has adopted several elements commonly associated with a "whole language" approach to reading and writing. A key element of this approach is that meaningful, authentic communication is the central focus of reading and writing (DeFord & Harste, 1982; Goodman & Goodman, 1981; Harste & Burke, 1977). As part of this approach, this teacher uses journal writing in which a daily period is set aside for students to communicate in writing with the teacher about virtually any topic the student selects. The teacher, of course, responds on a daily basis, and the journals are periodically collated and "published," serving as available reading material. The mechanics of the student's writing are not corrected, since the goal is to establish an authentic interaction through a written medium. Rather, the teacher's responses provide a model in which appropriate writing conventions are embedded in a whole, meaningful activity. In essence, the teacher's responses provide a zone of proximal development, through which the child is able to incorporate various elements into his or her own system of written communication.

Although a more extensive discussion of this research is available in Rueda, Flores, and Porter (1984), of prime interest in this work has been to track the development of writing skills over time. A data analysis form has been developed by the second author which allows the quantification and specification of elements of interest in writing samples, including both the mechanial aspects as well as functional aspects. In this scheme, it is possible to monitor not only mechanics such as handwriting, spelling, punctuation, capitalization, and grammar usage, but stylistic aspects as well (selection of topics, expansive vocabulary, complex sentences, stylistic variations, and revision strategies). Data from teacher interviews, as well as product data on the writing samples of the students in different contexts over time indicate that the students have begun to produce a different kind of writing than that previously found on drill type assignments. The students in this classroom have begun to create thoughtful narratives in a more coherent and complete fashion than had been evident on ditto sheets and on teacher-selected writing activities. In addition to these emerging findings, the students are acquiring writing skills, recorded in journal entries, which have never been formally instructed. That is, not only are students becoming proficient at producing creative and thematically related narratives, but they are demonstrating proficiency in the mechanical aspects of writing which are usually the main and often the only focus of writing instruction. In essence, the students in this project have demonstrated interest, motivation, and competence in the acquisition of writing through interaction in meaningful learning activities. That is, embedding writing in an interactional context where the communication of feelings and thoughts was the joint goal of the activity appeared to have the result of maximizing the acquisition of both the form and function of writing in a group of students for whom this is traditionally a difficult area of learning.

Discussion

The theoretical background which has been presented, as well as our work on literacy and the work of others, suggests the reconceptualization of the teaching and learning process into a more interactive framework than is traditionally adopted in schools. This is not to say that notions such as learning style do not exist or are not important. The cross-cultural research of Phillips (1972) and Erickson and Mohatt (1982), for example, demonstrate the impact of student interactional styles on classroom organization. Further, Au (1980) has described how cultural differences in interactional styles can be appropriated as a way of improving reading. Nevertheless, a more interactional notion of learning as mutually constructed activity appears to have much promise in the development of effective instructional options for children for whom teaching has traditionally been problematic.

A recent statement by Riel (1983) illustrates the point under discussion:

> Interaction is a constructive process in which participants engage in a process of creating understandings. These understandings form the mechanism of thought. Knowledge is activity and development is the process of internalizing and organizing these activity patterns. Since humans are essentially social, these activity patterns routinely involve interactions with others. Schools, however, often set up learning activities that are highly individualistic, thereby ignoring an important resource for learning." (p. 60)

In our current work, we have attempted to incorporate some of the theoretical principles discussed in an actual classroom situation. It is evident that a great deal of research remains to be completed. For example, data based upon the products of student's behavior, without specifying the processes by which they were created, permit only inferences and informed hypotheses. However, the preliminary findings indicate a great deal of promise in this framework which views learning as a social, interactive process. The final determination of the value of this theoretical framework depends upon further empirical demonstration. However, in light of the current concern with the education of handicapped children from diverse cultural backgrounds, and the often documented failure of current approaches, a critical examination of existing paradigms is warranted.

REFERENCES

Au, K. (1980). Participation structures in a reading lesson with Hawaiian children: Analysis of a culturally appropriate instruction event. <u>Anthropology and Education Quarterly</u>, <u>11</u>, 91-115.

Belmont, J. M., Ferretti, R. P., & Mitchell, D. W. (1982). Memorizing: A test of untrained mildly mentally retarded children's problem-solving. <u>American Journal of Mental Deficiency</u>, <u>87</u>, 197-210.

Ben-Zeev, S. (1972). <u>The influence of bilingualism on cognitive development and cognitive strategy.</u> Unpublished doctoral dissertation, University of Chicago.

Brooks, P. H., & Baumeister, A. A. (1977). A plea for consideration of ecological validity in the experimental psychology of mental retardation. <u>American Journal of Mental Deficiency</u>, <u>81</u>, 407-416.

Brown, A. L., & French, L. A. (1979). The zone of potential development: Implications for intelligence testing in the year 2000. <u>Intelligence</u>, <u>3</u>, 255-277.

Brown, R. L., Fournier, J. F., & Moyer, R. H. (1977). A cross cultural study of Piagetian concrete reasoning and science concepts among rural 5th grade Mexican and Anglo-American students. <u>Journal of Research in Science Teaching</u>, <u>14</u>, 329-334.

Campione, J. D., & Brown, A. L. (1977). Memory and meta-memory development in educable mentally retarded children. In R. V. Kail & J. W. Hagen (Eds.), <u>Perspective on the development of memory and cognition.</u> Hillsdale, NJ: Erlbaum Associates.

Cole, M., & Griffin, P. (1983). A socio-historical approach to remediation. <u>Quarterly Newsletter of the Laboratory of Comparative Human Cognition</u>, <u>5</u>(4), 69-74.

Cummins, J. (1978). Bilingualism and the development of metalinguistic awareness. <u>Journal of Cross-cultural Psychology</u>, <u>9</u>, 131-149.

Cummins, J., & Gulutsan, M. (1974). Bilingual education and cognition. <u>The Alberta Journal of Educational Research</u>, <u>20</u>, 259-269.

Darcy, N. T. (1963). Bilingualism and the measurement of intelligence: Review of a decade of research. <u>The Journal of Genetic Psychology</u>, <u>103</u>, 259-282.

DeAvila, E., & Duncan, S. E. (1981). Bilingualism and the metaset. In R. Duran (Ed.), <u>Latino language and communicative behavior.</u> Norwood NJ: Ablex Publishing Co.

DeAvila, E., & Pulos, S. M. (1979). Bilingualism and cognitive
development. In M. K. Poulsen & G. I. Lubin (Eds.), Piagetian
theory: The helping professions. Los Angeles: University of
Southern California.

De Ford, D. E., & Harste, J. (1982). Child language research and
curriculum. Language Arts, 59, 590-600.

Diaz, R. (1983). Thought and two languages: The impact of bilingualism
on cognitive development. In Review of Research of Education,
10, 23-54.

Duncan, S., & DeAvila, E. (1979). Bilingualism and cognition: Some
recent findings. NABE Journal, 4, 15-50.

Edgerton, R. B., & Langness, L. L. (1978). Observing mentally retarded
persons in community settings: An anthropological perspective. In
G. P. Sackett (Ed.), Observing behavior, Vol. 1: Theory and
applications in mental retardation. Baltimore: University Park
Press.

Erickson, F., & Mohatt, G. (1982). Cultural organization of
participation structures in two classrooms of Indian students. In G.
Spindler (Ed.), Doing the ethnography of schooling: Educational
anthropology in action. New York: Holt, Rinehart & Winston.

Feldman, C., & Shen, M. (1971). Some language related cognitive
advantage of bilingual five-year olds. Journal of Genetic
Psychology, 118, 235-244.

Goodman, K., & Goodman, Y. (1981). A whole-language
comprehension-centered view of reading development. Occasional
Paper No. 1. Tucson: Program in language and literacy, University
of Arizona.

Harste, J. C., & Burke, C. L. (1977). A new hypothesis for reading
teacher research: Both teaching and learning of reading are
theoretically based. In P. D. Pearson (Ed.), Reading: Theory,
research, practice. Twenty-sixth Yearbook of the National Reading
Conference. St. Paul MN: Mason Publishing Co.

Ianco-Worrall, A. (1972). Bilingualism and cognitive development.
Child Development, 43, 1390-1400.

Inhelder, B., & Piaget, J. (1971). Mental imagery in the child. New
York: Basic Books.

Jensen, J. V. (1962). Effects of childhood bilingualism. Elementary
English, 39, 132-143.

Kessler, C., & Quinn, M. E. (1979). Piaget and the bilingual child. In
M. K. Poulsen & G. I. Lubin (Eds.), Piagetian theory: The helping
professions. Los Angeles: University of Southern California.

Laboratory of Comparative Human Cognition. (1982). A model system for the study of learning difficulties. _Quarterly Newsletter of the Laboratory of Comparative Human Cognition_, _4_(3), 39-66.

Leopold, W. F. (1939-1949). _Speech development of a bilingual child. A linguist's record (4 Volumes)_. Evanston, IL: Northwestern University Press.

Levine, H., & Langness, L. L. (1983). _Everyday cognition among mildly retarded adults: An ethnographic approach_. Paper presented at the Annual Meeting of the American Association of Mental Deficiency, Dallas, Texas.

Liedtke, W. W., & Nelson, L. D. (1968). Concept formation and bilingualism. _Alberta Journal of Education Research_, _14_, 225-232.

McDermott, R. P. (1977). Social relations as contexts for learning in school. _Harvard Educational Review_, _47_, 298-313.

Mehan, H. (1978). Structuring school structure. _Harvard Educational Review_, _45_, 311-338.

Mehan, H. (1979). _Learning lessons: Social organization in the classroom_. Cambridge, MA: Harvard University Press.

Osherson, D. E., & Markham, E. (1975). Language and the ability to evaluate contradictions and tautologies. _Cognition_, _3_, 213-226.

Peal, E., & Lambert, W. E. (1962). The relation of bilingualism to intelligence. _Psychological Monographs: General and Applied_, _76_, 1-23.

Phillips, S. (1972). Participant structures and communicative competence. In C. B. Cazden, V. P. John, & D. Hymes, (Eds.), _Functions of language in the classroom_. New York: Teachers College Press.

Price-Williams, D., & Gallimore, R. (1980). The cultural perspective. In B. Keogh (Ed.), _Advances in special education_, Vol. 2. JAI Press.

Riel, M. (1983). Education and ecstasy: Computer chronicles of students writing together. _Quarterly Newsletter of the Laboratory of Comparative Human Cognition_, _5_(3), 59-67.

Rueda, R. (1983). Cognitive development and bilingualism in exceptional and non-exceptional children. In J. Bransford (Ed.), _Bueno Center for Multicultural Education Monograph Series_, _4_(1), 1-45.

Rueda, R., & Flores, B. (1984). <u>Literacy development in a special education classroom with bilingual students</u>. Paper presented at the Arizona Association for Bilingual Education Annual Conference, Flagstaff, AZ, March.

Rueda, R., Flores, B., & Porter, B. (1984). <u>Aspects of literacy and social interaction in a special education classroom with bilingual students</u>. Manuscript submitted for publication.

Rueda, R., & Mehan, H. (1984). <u>Metacognition and passing: A context specific interpretation of learning disabilities</u>. Manuscript submitted for publication.

Schultz, J., Florio, S., & Erickson, F. (1980). "Where's the floor?": Aspects of the cultural organization of social relationships in communication at home and at school. In P. Gillmore (Ed.), <u>Ethnography and education: Children in and out of school</u>. Georgetown: Center for Applied Linguistics.

Vygotsky, L. S. (1978). <u>Mind in society</u>. Cambridge MA: Harvard University Press.

Wertsch, J. (1981). <u>The concept of activity in Soviet Psychology</u>. New York: M. E. Sharpe.

Whitaker, J. H., Rueda, R., & Prieto, A. (1984). <u>Cognitive performance as a function of bilingualism in mildly retarded students</u>. Manuscript submitted for publication.

Yela, M. (1975). Comprension verbal y bilingualismo. <u>Revista de Psicologia General y Aplicado</u>, <u>30</u>, 1045.

CHAPTER 4

LANGUAGE AND CURRICULUM DEVELOPMENT
FOR EXCEPTIONAL BILINGUAL CHILDREN

Alba A. Ortiz

In 1979, Chinn conducted extensive literature searches in an effort to identify specialized curricula for handicapped culturally different children. These searches yielded publications which addressed strategies and approaches appropriate to minorities, but none were specific to exceptional children. Five years later, Chinn's work remains state of the art: (a) There are few, if any, curricula designed for exceptional culturally diverse students; (b) few instructional strategies have universal appeal and utilitarian value; (c) frequently, it is individual teachers who develop curricula and instructional strategies for use with these students; and (d) there has been little dissemination of available curricula, materials, and instructional strategies for this population.

The lack of information related to handicapped minorities is even more dramatic when one considers educational programming for exceptional language-minority students. Special education literature rarely discusses unique considerations in working with limited-English-proficient (LEP) or bilingual students.

It is the purpose of this article to highlight emerging issues and concerns associated with language and curriculum development for exceptional bilingual students and to review literature which holds promise in developing practice and policy for service delivery to these students.

BILINGUAL INSTRUCTION FOR THE HANDICAPPED

A common misconception is that handicapped children who have limited English proficiency, or who are bilingual, should be taught in English. Educators reason that if exceptional children have difficulty developing language skills, they will require more time than others to master a language and will be confused by bilingual instruction. It is thought to be in the best interest of students to provide instruction in one language and the choice is usually English (Ortiz, 1984). Cummins

(1982), however, suggests that bilingual instruction is more effective than English-only instruction in promoting English academic skills and that native language skills can be developed without negative repercussions for the learning of English. As a matter of fact, the greater the child's proficiency in his or her native language, the greater likelihood of success in learning English as a second language.

Baca (1980) provides an historical overview of litigation and legislation related to the education of LEP children and establishes a strong case for bilingual education as a sound instructional method. Studies cited indicated that bilinguals are better able to deal with abstract aspects of language, have greater cognitive flexibility, and may have greater linguistic sensitivity. Rather than being cognitively or academically impaired, children learning two languages may have skills superior to those of monolinguals (Albert & Obler, 1978).

While there are many questions regarding bilingual development to be resolved by future research, a growing body of literature suggests that bilingual proficiency is not beyond the capability of handicapped children and that a policy of single-language instruction may ignore linguistic skills which are important to the child and to his or her community (Greenlee, 1981). Several studies document student improvement or gains in achievement as a result of native language, English as a second language, or bilingual education strategies with handicapped LEP students:

1. Askins (1978) found that students involved in the Responsive Environment Early Education Program (REEEP) made significant gains in language development both in English and Spanish and in school readiness. Sixty percent of the students scored better than estimated/expected on a test of English; 40% scored better than estimated/expected on a test of Spanish.

2. In a study of intellectually and physically handicapped children, Sanua (1976) found that 78% of the subjects showed progress in reading and 74% showed gains in self-concept when instruction was conducted bilingually.

3. Baca (1974) found that informal and structured bilingual interventions resulted in improvement of attitudes and achievement among 15 mildly handicapped students.

4. Weiss (1980) documented dramatic language-related learning improvement among 3- to 5-year-old handicapped children participating in the INreal REactive Language (INREAL) program. Longitudinal data showed that students who had participated in the project had less need for follow-up remedial services and fewer grade retentions.

5. McConnell (1981) describes the use of Individualized Bilingual Instruction (IBI) for teaching academic areas and oral language in English and in Spanish. Gains for both high- and low-ability children were educationally and statistically significant.

6. Observations, interviews with participating teachers, and data from a survey questionnaire (Muller, 1975) indicated that, through bilingual approach, bilingual mentally retarded students were able to improve communication and study skills and were able to develop better teacher/student rapport.

7. Bruck (1978), who studied the suitability of early French immersion programs for the learning disabled child, found that children with language problems in French immersion programs continued to develop facility in their first language, learned basic skills at the predicted rate, and exhibited no severe behavioral problems.

The instructional process for language-minority students who have learning difficulties should be consistent with what we know about how language is acquired and about the interrelationships between first and second language acquisition. For minority students who are academically at risk, strong promotion of native language conceptual skills will be more effective in providing a basis for the acquisition of literacy in English (Cummins, 1983).

Language Choice

Secada (in press) offers a framework for choosing language interventions for hearing-impaired Hispanics which includes the major options available for limited-English-proficient students (use of English or the native language only; use of two languages, the native language and ESL; exclusive use of the native language) and the major program options for the hearing impaired (exclusive use of oral English; a mixture of oral and manual communication; exclusive use of the manual mode). By increasing program options, students might, for example, receive content instruction in the native language, English as a second language training to enhance transfer of oral skills from the native language to English, and as training in total communication to facilitate mainstreaming. Secada cautions that programs that develop English oral or manual sign skills to the exclusion of students' home language risk confusing and alienating them from their community.

Adequate instruments and models have yet to be developed to capture the complex relationship between first and second language acquisition or to describe the relationship between variables such as attitudes and motivations of second language learners to attained language proficiency (Johnson & Krug, 1980). The task of sorting out these relationships becomes even more complex with the addition of a handicapping condition. Nonetheless, careful consideration must be given to factors which might influence the child's performance and affect language choice, including (a) parent choice or preference; (b) student choice or preference; (c) student age; (d) length of time in this country; (e) type and severity of handicapping condition; (f) language aptitude; (g) general intellectual abilities; (h) motivation; (i) attitudes toward speakers of English and toward instruction in English or the other language; (j) time allocated to language teaching and to instructional tasks; (k) performance or progress as a result of instruction in a given language; and (l) availability of bilingual personnel, and so forth. Because of the multiplicity of variables which must be considered in choosing the language of instruction, a significant contribution to the field would be the development of a framework for weighing these variables in educational/instructional decision-making.

Cultural Relevance in Curriculum

Perhaps the most common theme in the literature is that poor achievement can be attributed to content, materials, and strategies which are not culturally relevant (Almanza & Mosley, 1980; Chinn, 1979a; Diggs, 1974; Jaramillo, 1974; Ortiz, 1981; Plata, 1979; Rodriguez, Cole, Stile, & Gallegos, 1979). While there is general agreement that adapting curricula and materials to make them culturally relevant is a step toward reducing the discrepancy between the characteristics of the student and those of school programs, there is disagreement about the nature of cultural differences which must be considered, their distribution within given groups, and specifically how instruction should be adapted to take these factors into account (Henderson, 1980). Benson (as cited in Benson, Medrich, & Buckley, 1980) summarizes this dilemma:

> Each year children attend school, they bring with them a lot of "baggage": their health, energy levels, knowledge of skills acquired in formal learning and in informal activities, tastes, attitudes, and expectations. Presumably, some of this baggage is helpful to a given child in his school work, and some is not helpful. We know very little about how the baggage is acquired by a child, or in some cases, forced on him. What we do know is that the differences in school performance of children is greater than can be explained by initial intellectual endowments and that the gap in performance tends to get wider the longer children attend school....So public policy, as it has shaped up, seeks to compensate for deficiencies in home background but this compensation is offered in the absence of knowledge of precisely what, if anything, is lacking in the home toward which compensation should be made. (pp. 174-175)

The most frequent recommendation found in the literature urges educators to incorporate the history, heritage, traditions, and lifestyles of diverse cultural groups when developing or adapting instructional materials or curricula. However, when emphasis is given to traditional aspects of culture, instructional materials may inadvertently reinforce the very stereotypes and misperceptions educators wish to eliminate. Educators must learn as much as possible about the contemporary culture of students and create learning environments and curricula which are compatible with student characteristics, with expectations and desires of parents and community, and which are consistent with public policy. Cultural relevance, coupled with sound special education techniques, can provide a basic foundation for meeting the needs of exceptional minorities (Chinn, 1979b).

Henderson (1980) provides an overview of basic concepts related to cultural diversity and stereotypes associated with cultural and social variables and their influence on student performance. He concludes that the only variables consistently related to achievement are level of student involvement in academic tasks, the nature of teacher-pupil interactions, and internal perceptions of control.

Student Involvement

Recently, researchers have begun to address teacher behavior and pupil learning styles and their correlation with achievement of bilingual students. Preliminary findings of the Significant Bilingual Instruction Features study (Tikunoff, 1982) indicate that teaching behaviors of bilingual education teachers compared favorably with literature on effective instruction and particularly with studies which indicate that students make the most significant learning gains when they receive a great deal of instruction from, and interaction with, the teacher. The SBIF study showed that during effective bilingual instruction, teachers communicated clearly and engaged students in task completion; organized instructional activities which created, reinforced, and communicated task and instruction demands; monitored students' work; and provided frequent and immediate feedback. Teachers also mediated instruction using both English and the native language and responded to and used cultural clues. Under these conditions, LEP students were successful in understanding new information and task expectations and in obtaining accurate feedback regarding their performance. Evidence of this achievement was high academic learning time, time spent in a particular content area engaged in learning tasks with a high degree of accuracy. The SBIF findings are consistent with literature that suggests that when pupils have opportunities to express their ideas, and when their ideas are incorporated into learning activities, pupils seem to learn more and to develop more positive attitudes toward the teacher and learning (Silvernail, 1979).

Internal Perceptions of Control

The concept of locus of control, originally formulated by Rotter (1966), describes a person's perceptions of the relationship between actions and outcomes. "Internals" believe they are in control of their lives and that work and effort will result in reward. "Externals" believe outcomes are determined by luck, chance, fate, or powerful others who control their destinies in random fashion. Locus of control appears to be partially a function of socioeconomic status, as frequently poor or economically disadvantaged individuals are likely to demonstrate characteristics of externals (Henderson, 1980; Ortiz & Yates, 1982; Vasquez, 1975).

An external orientation may have devastating effects upon achievement of minority children. For example, some externals will have difficulty processing information and profiting from instruction presented from a framework of independence and intrinsic motivation. Additionally, externals are unlikely to analyze feedback accurately to determine how to change their behavior to become more successful within the school system

(Ortiz & Yates, 1984). Instead, external children begin to perceive themselves as helpless and unable to control what happens to them, and to see aversive situations as insurmountable. They fail to perceive their own effort as an important cause of success or failure. This sets into play teacher perceptions and expectations which maintain the cycle of failure and reinforce the learned helplessness (Henderson, 1980).

There is a striking parallel between the characteristics of children with external locus of control orientations and those attributes associated with learning disabled students. Consequently, guidance is needed to determine when children are experiencing school-related difficulties because of lack of compatibility between teaching and learning styles or when such difficulties would best be attributed to a handicapping condition.

Teacher-Pupil Interactions

Teacher expectations are the inferences or predictions teachers make about the present and future academic achievement and general classroom behavior of their pupils. When teachers hold positive perceptions and expectations, they provide increased quality of educational opportunity (Good & Brophy, 1973). Individuals labeled underachievers may become victims of lowered expectations for achievement and these expectations may negatively affect instructional opportunities (Rist, 1970).

Conversely, as the quality of instruction is diminished, over time, the quality of instruction alone could explain differences in achievement levels of children. Such a conclusion is significant given evidence which indicates that minorities lag far behind their peers in academic achievement (Brown, Rosen, Hill, & Olivas, 1980). Research associated with teacher-pupil interaction patterns and teaching styles and behaviors has not routinely included handicapped students, much less the handicapped LEP child. The majority of studies of exceptional individuals focus on the effects of handicapping condition on teacher perceptions, expectations, and interactions. Research has yet to determine the effects of differential interaction and teaching style patterns on the achievement of LEP populations or the interaction effects of linguistic/cultural diversity and handicapping conditions.

PROMISING PRACTICES

Useful Models

Adelman (cited in Hammill & Bartel, 1971) suggests a two-step process for educating students experiencing achievement problems. The first step is to personalize the instructional environment so compatibility between student charcteristics and teaching/learning styles is attained. The second step requires that instruction be carefully sequenced in such a way that the student is ready to learn the content or concepts presented.

Using models such as Adelman's provides assurance that the environment has been personalized, making it more likely that children will not be inappropriately referred to special education on the basis of learning problems which could best be attributed to failure to accommodate individual differences. Sequencing instruction and the use of significantly different instructional strategies provide a number of opportunities to improve student performance before a referral to special education is made. Once a referral is made, documentation of prior interventions provides valuable data, not only for assessment purposes, but also for development of an individual education plan if the child is eligible for special education.

Lerman and Cortez (1978) provide a comprehensive model, illustrated in Figure 1, for discovering and meeting the needs of handicapped children from dual language backgrounds. While this model was developed for the hearing impaired, variables considered are generally applicable to all categories of handicapping condition and provide an excellent framework for personalizing instruction.

FIGURE 1
Variables Affecting Language Functioning

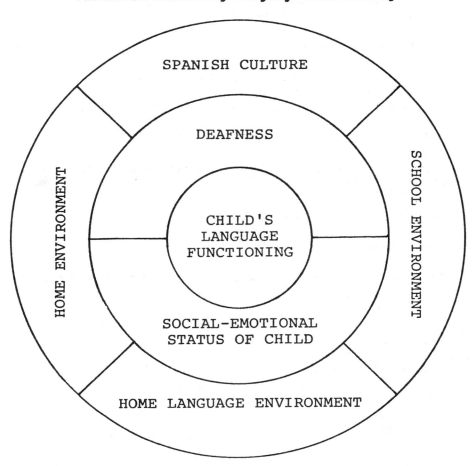

Note. From A. Lerman and E. Cortez. (1978). <u>Discovering and meeting the</u> <u>needs of Hispanic hearing impaired children</u>. ERIC Document Reproduction Service No. ED 155-292.

Areas included in the model include the following:

I. Language status of the child

    A. Language used by the child

    B. Child's mode of communication in language(s) used

    C. Competence in language(s) and modes

II. Social-emotional station of the child (e.g., social interaction, success, school adjustment)

III. Culture

    A. Background and family (e.g., identification with national origin, status in country of origin)

    B. Factors affecting parents' functioning with the child (e.g., roles, discipline)

IV. Home language environment

    A. Patterns of communication in the family (e.g., competence, language used with child, amount of communication, attitudes toward learning English)

    B. Avenues of communication in the home

    C. Patterns of residence (e.g., travel between U. S. and native country)

    D. Language of materials in the home

V. Home environment

    A. Description of family members (e.g., general characteristics, major caregivers, parent's education, place of birth or childhood)

    B. Patterns of residence

    C. Economic factors

    D. Neighborhood

    E. The family and institutions (e.g., contacts, use)

VI. School environment

    A. Patterns of school enrollment (e.g., number of years in school, where, attendance)

B. School's accommodation of bilingual or LEP children and
    families (e.g., percentage in the school, number of bilingual
    personnel, school language programs)

C. Teacher's relationship with the child

VII. Handicapping condition

A. General consideration (e.g., etiology, age of onset)

B. Role of parents (e.g., initial reactions, present attitudes)

The components of the model become the critical data for effective
IEP development.

Instruction Strategies

Ambert and Dew (1982) suggest that IEPs for bilingual children include a
language use plan designating what subjects or skills will be taught in
which language, and specifying the language of instruction for each
objective in the plan. Recommendations for instructional strategies,
techniques, and materials which are linguistically relevant and
appropriate to the handicapping condition must be identified; appropriate
reinforcers and motivators should be specified. The following strategies
and approaches appear to have potential for improving practice in
instruction of handicapped bilingual students.

Second Language Acquisition. Children _acquire_ as opposed to _learn_, a
second language by understanding messages, not by focusing on linguistic
form or analyzing structures as is frequently done in language teaching
(Krashen, 1982). Contrary to popular belief, increased exposure to
English does not improve or hasten second language acquisition.
Consequently, submersion or "sink-or-swim" programs in which children are
simply placed in the same classroom with native English speakers and the
regular curriculum is followed will not be successful. Adding English as
a Second Language instruction to the submersion program will help but the
most effective program is one in which subject matter is taught in the
native language and a source of comprehensible English input is provided.

Based on their studies of second language acquisition, Dulay, Burt,
and Krashen (1982) provide the following guidelines for teaching English
as a second language:

1. Maximize the student's exposure to natural communication.

2. Focus on the message being conveyed, not the linguistic form of the
    message.

3. Incorporate a silent period at the beginning of the instructional
    program so that students will be able to listen to the second
    language without being pressured to speak it.

4. Encourage and create situations in which students can interact with native speakers of the language.

5. Use concrete referents to make the new language understandable to beginning students.

6. Devise specific techniques to relax students and to protect their egos. The less anxious, more motivated, more self-confident students experience greater success in second language acquisition (Krashen, 1982).

7. Learn the motivations of students and incorporate these into lessons.

8. Create an atmosphere where students are not embarrassed by their errors.

9. Do not refer to, or revert to, the student's native language when teaching the second language. To do so may create a situation in which the student, instead of focusing attention on the second language, simply waits for the teacher to repeat utterances in the native language. Under these circumstances, motivation for second language learning may be negatively affected.

Language acquisition takes place best when input is provided that is (a) comprehensible; (b) interesting and relevant; (c) not grammatically sequenced; and (e) provided in suffecent quantity (Krashen, 1982). Krashen uses these criteria to evaluate methods for language teaching. Traditional methods such as audio-lingual, grammar-translation, and cognitive code methods do not do an effective job of encouraging subconscious language acquisition. The following methods provide comprehensive input and thus facilitate language acquisition (National Clearinghouse for Bilingual Education, 1984):

1. The Total Physical Response approach (Asher, 1979) develops language comprehension through student's body movements. Commands are given in the second language and acted out first by teachers and then by students, allowing students to perceive the meaning of the commands while hearing the language.

2. Suggestopedia (Bushman & Madsen, 1976), a method developed by Georgi Lozanov, uses nonverbal techniques, classical music, and aesthetic surroundings to provide a comfortable ambience for language learning.

3. The natural approach (Krashen & Terrell, 1983) encourages language acquisition by developing proficiency without direct or conscious recourse to the formal rules of the language and focuses on successful expression of meaning rather than on correctness of form.

These methods seem to be more effective than traditional approaches because they provide time for students to develop comprehension skills, attempt to reduce student anxiety, and provide a source of comprehensible input. For handicapped students, these methods offer simplified language codes and active involvement in the learning process, sound special education teaching principles.

Instrumental Enrichment. Harth (1982) suggests that traditional special education interventions, because they are based on the assumption that low functioning individuals are not modifiable, are designed to prepare individuals to function at low levels. These programs "mold the requirements and activities of the educational setting to fit the student's level of functioning. Thus the student's educational program prepares him or her to function in a marginal, perhaps semi-dependent environment" (p. 1).

Feuerstein (1980) reasons that retarded performance of children may be the result of lack of mediated learning experiences (MLE), rather than lack of interaction with the environment. Too few mediated experiences can result in poor thinking skills which, in turn, reduce the individual's ability to learn from further direct experiences. Neither remedial efforts aimed at providing a stimulating environment nor emphasis on traditional academics will be effective in overcoming cognitive deficiencies. Instead, there is the need to mediate learning experiences, that is, to intervene between the person and the environment and to transform, reorder, organize, group, and frame the stimuli in the direction of some specifically intended goal and purpose.

Feuerstein's (1980) Instrumental Enrichment (FIE) program is designed to mediate experiences by making the individual more receptive and sensitive to internal and external sources of stimulation. This approach is directed, not only at remediation of specific behaviors and skills, but also at changing the person's manner of interacting with, acting on, or responding to sources of information. Tasks are structured in such a way that they require the student to: (a) use higher mental processes; (b) develop intrinsic motivation through formation of habits; and (c) contribute actively to the organization, restructuring, discovery, and application of produced relationships. In essence, what the student is doing is learning to learn.

Feuerstein identifies "flaws" in basic thinking skills among slow learners including: (a) impulsivity; (b) failure to recognize problems; (c) episodic grasps of reality -- that is, events and objects are viewed in isolation; (d) failure to make comparisons; and (e) inadequate spatial orientation (Chance, 1981). Retarded performers fail to recognize that their own intellectual efforts may contribute to solution of the problem and, instead, see themselves simply as recipients of information. There is a striking similarity between these "flaws" and characteristics attributed to children with an external locus of control.

The literature suggests that minority group children and children from lower socioeconomic status environments are likely to be externals. The literature is also replete with reports that externals are likely to be underachievers. Henderson (1980) suggests that teachers provide external students with opportunities to set goals and to help determine their own activities. Cognitively oriented attribution retraining and environmental control and self-regulation programs can be used to teach cause-effect relationships. If it is indeed possible to train thinking skills, the academic performance of minority students could be significantly improved through the use of the FIE. Findings of several studies conducted in this country show positive effects for the use of the FIE; students who have had this training show a slight advantage over control groups on varied measures of intelligence and these gains seem to hold over time. Chance (1981) cautions, however, that there is not a sufficient body of carefully controlled research available demonstrating that students do indeed benefit from instrumental enrichment. The use of the FIE is a promising area for research related to best practices in intervention for minority students, including exceptional language minorities.

Educational Implications of Hemispheric Research. Studies of cerebral organization for language suggest that language is organized in the brain of bilingual individuals in a manner that is different from that of monolinguals. Research with monolingual subjects has indicated that the left hemisphere is dominant for language in most individuals; studies of bilinguals suggest that the right hemisphere plays a major role in the learning of a second language (Albert & Obler, 1978). It is possible that early emphasis on one hemisphere can lead to permanent cognitive deficits.

Rubenzer (1979) suggests that, instead of focusing on improving curricula, emphasis should be given to increasing students' receptivity (meta-skills) to learning experiences and materials. In the classroom, balanced approaches to teaching should be used, teaching toward both the left and the right hemispheres. While the brain is "bifunctional," the most productive and creative intellectual funtioning is theorized to occur when there is cooperation between hemispheres. Educational experiences specifically designed to enhance right brain processing also improve performance on left hemisphere tasks. Shifts in the quality and focus of attention can be consciously elicited and the most advantageous cognitive and effective modes can be consciously attained apropos the stage of problem solving at hand. Patterns found to best facilitate problem solving can then be practiced.

Materials and Media. Results of a questionnaire by Bland, Sabatino, Sedlack, and Sterberg (1979) indicate a general agreement among respondents that learner characteristics of minority and handicapped children require specially developed curricula and alternative modes of presentation. However, even when available, media and materials developed specifically for these children must be adapted because they are not suitable; i.e., they lack relevance to the student's background, fail to accommodate linguistic characteristics, and/or reflect cultural bias. This is particularly true of academic subjects requiring reading, language development, prevocational skills, and affective social instruction.

Teachers have little recourse other than to improvise or to adapt materials developed for handicapped or for bilingual students. Criteria for evaluation of materials must include a description of their characteristics; cultural relevance; effect of adaptation on content, intent, or objectives of materials; and differences associated with student learning styles (DeLeon, 1983). DeLeon also suggests viewing the classroom as an ecological system so that materials evaluation would include analysis of the curriculum, the student, the teacher, and the physical environment in which the student must perform.

Service Delivery Models

Handicapped children should have access to the same types of placement options as are provided handicapped monolingual English speakers. This right is frequently ignored when placement decisions are made for LEP students because of the common misconception that, if they are handicapped, these students should be removed from a bilingual instructional setting and placed in a totally English language curriculum. As has been discussed, such reasoning ignores that native language proficiency will determine level of success in acquiring English skills (Cummins, 1981). Placement in special language programs should be continued, if appropriate, and teachers should be provided assistance in adapting classroom programs to meet the child's special education needs.

A major problem in determining appropriate educational placements for handicapped bilingual students is the shortage of special education personnel who are bilingual and who have specialized training related to serving exceptional limited-English-proficient or bilingual students. The majority of LEP or bilingual students are served by native English speakers who use the same instructional strategies and procedures as are used with monolingual English speaking students. Consequently, educational prescriptions often fail to yield desired results as they do not accommodate student differences across variables such as language and culture.

School districts have begun to explore alternative service delivery models for bilingual students. Figure 2 illustrates three models which allow the integration of specialized curriculum in the first or second language and mainstreaming to either a bilingual education or a regular education program (Ambert & Dew, 1982).

FIGURE 2
Service Delivery Options for Exceptional Bilingual Students

BILINGUAL SUPPORT MODEL

SPECIAL EDUCATION TEACHER (Monolingual)

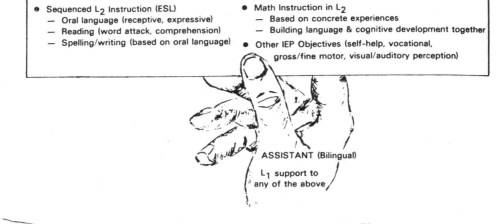

- Sequenced L_2 Instruction (ESL)
  - Oral language (receptive, expressive)
  - Reading (word attack, comprehension)
  - Spelling/writing (based on oral language)
- Math Instruction in L_2
  - Based on concrete experiences
  - Building language & cognitive development together
- Other IEP Objectives (self-help, vocational, gross/fine motor, visual/auditory perception)

ASSISTANT (Bilingual)

L_1 support to any of the above

COORDINATED SERVICES MODEL

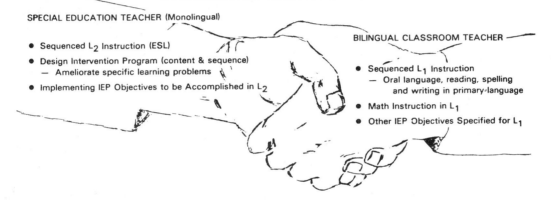

SPECIAL EDUCATION TEACHER (Monolingual)

- Sequenced L_2 Instruction (ESL)
- Design Intervention Program (content & sequence)
  - Ameliorate specific learning problems
- Implementing IEP Objectives to be Accomplished in L_2

BILINGUAL CLASSROOM TEACHER

- Sequenced L_1 Instruction
  - Oral language, reading, spelling and writing in primary language
- Math Instruction in L_1
- Other IEP Objectives Specified for L_1

INTEGRATED BILINGUAL SPECIAL EDUCATION MODEL

BILINGUAL SPECIAL EDUCATION TEACHER

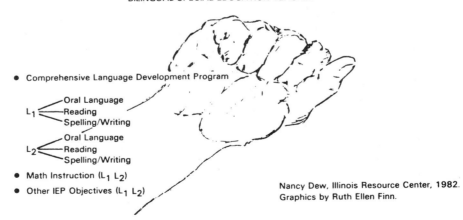

- Comprehensive Language Development Program

L_1 — Oral Language / Reading / Spelling/Writing

L_2 — Oral Language / Reading / Spelling/Writing

- Math Instruction (L_1 L_2)
- Other IEP Objectives (L_1 L_2)

Nancy Dew, Illinois Resource Center, 1982.
Graphics by Ruth Ellen Finn.

Note. From A. Ambert and N. Dew, <u>Special education for exceptional bilingual students: A handbook for educators</u> (Milwaukee WI: Midwest National Origin Desegregation Assistance Center, 1982), p. 85.

Bilingual Support Model. Bilingual paraprofessionals are teamed with monolingual English-speaking special educators and assist with the implementation of objectives specified in the IEP. The special education teacher provides English as a Second Language instruction in basic skills areas in English. Caution is exercised to ensure that the linguistic requirements of academic tasks are consistent with the child's English language development. Instruction in subjects such as math are based on concrete experiences and build language and cognitive development together. The teacher assistant provides native language instruction in areas specified in the IEP as requiring native language instruction.

The bilingual support model has the obvious advantage that the child has access to someone who speaks his or her language. If bilingual paraprofessionals received training specific to the responsibilities and tasks they are asked to perform, they become invaluable resources for the monolingual teacher. Without access to such personnel, children may essentially be denied appropriate educational opportunities.

Coordinated Services Model. Under this model, handicapped LEP students are served by a team consisting of a monolingual English speaking special education teacher and a bilingual educator. The special educator provides ESL instruction and is responsible for implementing IEP objectives to be accomplished in English. The bilingual education teacher provides sequenced instruction in the basic skills areas (oral language, math, reading, spelling, writing, etc.) in the native language and is reponsible for services designated in the IEP which are to be provided in the native language.

The benefit of this model is that handicapped children have access to personnel trained in the complementary disciplines of bilingual education and special education. These teachers meet to review student progress and revise instructional programs accordingly. Another advantage is that bilingual educators may be able to facilitate parental involvement in decisions affecting their child's education.

The coordinated services model may not be cost-effective. Two teachers are required to serve handicapped LEP students in special education classrooms. Unless a district has large numbers of children requiring special education services in a language other than English, this model is not likely to be used.

Integrated Bilingual Special Education Model. This model is used when a district has teachers who are trained in both bilingual education and special education. These dually certified teachers provide special education instruction in the native language, provide English as a second language training, and assist in the transition into English language instruction as the child develops adequate proficiency. Instruction is adapted to meet the specific needs associated with the nature and severity of the handicapping condition. This model, while it may be cost-effective, is seldom used because of the scarcity of teachers with training in both fields.

Bilingual Special Education Model. Ortiz and Yates (1982) suggest a fourth model based on the premise that teachers who serve handicapped LEP students require more than training in bilingual education and special education. Rather, there is a unique body of knowledge supportive of, and unique to, bilingual special education. To illustrate this concept, a teacher who is knowledgeable about programming for mentally retarded students, and who has been trained in bilingual education, many not be able to bring together these knowledge bases to develop an appropriate educational program for the mentally retarded LEP student. Bilingual special education teachers are those who have been exposed to and have developed competencies specific to servicing exceptional bilingual students. There are few such personnel available because there are few bilingual special education training programs and because there is little research available specific to LEP handicapped children. Many of the unique aspects of bilingual special education are yet to be identified.

All four models require, at some point, interdisciplinary teams for service delivery. Members of the team contribute their unique expertise, experience, and training, facilitating an interface among bilingual education, special education, regular education, and related programs. Educators participating in coordinated efforts must be provided opportunities to develop increased awareness and skills to ensure that LEP children are afforded appropriate educational programs and services. Categories of instructional personnel who should be targeted for training include the following (Ortiz & Yates, 1982):

Bilingual education teachers. These teachers are serving (a) children who are handicapped but who have not been referred because of the lack of bilingual special education teachers or because bilingual educators lack skills to identify children who should be referred to special education and (b) children who are handicapped and who have been mainstreamed into their classes. Bilingual educators frequently lack training to help exceptional children achieve their potential in the context of the regular classroom.

Special education teachers who are bilingual. One should not assume that if a teacher is bilingual and has special education training, he or she can serve exceptional LEP children effectively. These individuals should not necessarily be considered bilingual/special education teachers, but only special education teachers who are bilingual. This is a critical distinction and only those teachers who have received training in both bilingual and special education should be considered bilingual/special education teachers. Training in areas such as how to provide native language instruction and how to adapt such instruction to meet children's special education needs can increase the effectiveness of services provided by these teachers.

Monolingual special education teachers. As indicated previously, the reality is that the majority of exceptional bilingual children are served by monolingual English speaking special education personnel. Effectiveness of services is increased when teachers are provided training relative to factors which influence the performance of LEP students and on how to provide instruction in English which is comprehensible and relevant given the language, culture, and other attributes of this population. Training in English as a Second Language techniques and methods is important for these personnel.

Regular classroom teachers. Overrepresentation of LEP students in language-related categories (Garcia, 1983; Maldonado, 1984; Ortiz & Yates, 1983) suggests that teachers are unable to distinguish linguistic/cultural differences from handicapping conditions. Training of regular educators may result in more appropriate referrals to special education and in the provision of more appropriate education programs in mainstream settings. Of particular concern is that regular classroom teachers continue to provide language support for students who are exited from special language programs to ensure they have adequate English proficiency to perform academic tasks successfully (Cummins, 1981; Ortiz, 1984).

Paraprofessionals. There is a need to train paraprofessionals who, in many instances, will have primary responsibility for instructing the handicapped LEP child. Unless these personnel receive training specific to the responsibilities and tasks they are required to perform, handicapped LEP children may essentially be denied educational opportunities. Content for training of paraprofessionals would include competencies associated with general education procedures, competencies to provide native language instruction and English as a second language instruction, and skills to adapt instruction to the needs of the handicapped learner.

Assessment personnel. There is a scarcity of assessment personnel who can test the child in his or her native language and interpret performance in light of the student's background characteristics. Consequently, children may be inaccurately diagnosed as handicapped because appraisal services appropriate both in terms of the handicapping condition and specific student characteristics are not available.

Administrators. As indicated earlier, coordination between bilingual education and special language programs is critical to serving bilingual exceptional students. This coordination would not, for many schools, require reorganization of programs and services, but rather establishment of mechanisms for ensuring coordination of effort. It is the responsibility of administrators, particularily principals and supervisors, to ensure that necessary services are provided, adequate resources are allocated, and instructional interventions recommended are implemented (Ortiz & Yates, 1982). Assisting and/or training administrators in program management strategies would be beneficial in achieving bilingual education-special education interfaces.

Other support personnel. Personnel in related services areas such as counseling, physical and occupational therapy, adaptive physical education, etc. should also be provided training in order to allow their actions and decisions related to LEP handicapped students to be rational, data based, and appropriate. Parents need assurance that they can be effective and informed participants in decision making processes related to their children's education. To develop such effectiveness, they need training related to the school milieu, school policies, and procedures, instructional options, and so forth.

SUMMARY

The literature does not directly address the need for <u>new</u> curricula and instructional methods for bilingual exceptional students. This may be due to the paucity of empirical research on this topic. It would be premature to conclude that existing curricula and materials can meet the needs of this population. Until such research is available, research conducted in related disciplines will continue to provide the basis for educational programming decisions. As new research findings are produced and disseminated, practices should be modified or adapted as appropriate.

Already in place is evidence that bilingual education and special education can be linked together in effective problem solving formats. It is possible to describe instructional arrangements being used for bilingual exceptional students, but there is little empirical evidence available to determine the most appropriate arrangement(s) for any given handicapping condition or identified student characteristics.

A major issue is whether handicapped students should receive dual language instruction. Educators wonder whether it may be more effective, when an LEP student is eligible for special education, to remove that student from a bilingual education placement and place him or her in a classroom where instruction is provided solely in English. Literature on second language acquisition would not support this decision. There is growing evidence that handicapped children, just like normal children, receive the most appropriate education when they are provided instruction in their native language, participate in a structured program fr learning English if appropriate, and when instruction is consonant with both the handicapping conditions and student background characteristics.

There is a need to develop instructional materials and curricula and to make them available to educators who serve exceptional LEP students. This is not an awesome task in that much groundwork has already been done in identifying existing materials which may be appropriate to this population or which could be adapted to meet specific student needs or characteristics (Dew, 1981; Deignan & Ryen, 1979). It would not be accurate, then, to say that there are no materials on the market. However, information about resources which do exist has not been disseminated widely.

It is questionable whether it is possible to leave responsibility for adapting or modifying curricula or materials to existing school personnel. There is a general lack of understanding of linguistically and culturally different populations, even in settings where minorities comprise the majority student body (Maldonado, 1984; Garcia, 1984). Because of the lack of data readily available, teachers and others would not be able, on an ongoing basis, to adapt instructional materials and strategies to make them relevant in terms of LEP student characteristics and instructional goals. Appropriately trained staff could address this issue. However, as indicated previously, few institutions of higher education or related agencies currently address the needs of bilingual special education populations in the context of teacher preparation programs. Institutions which provide preservice bilingual special education training programs do not have the capability to meet manpower needs for bilingual special educators. Further, it is unlikely that adequate resources would be allocated to provide the required in-depth inservice training to currently employed personnel.

What emerges is a critical need for networking of efforts. State education agencies, local school districts, institutions of higher education, regional or intermediate agencies, must all become sensitized to the issues or concerns, allowing a broad-based inclusion of training, policy formulation, and procedures which focus upon the needs of LEP handicapped students. Without such a focus, an increasing percentage of this country's most critical resources, its youth, will remain unavailable to the required futures of the nation.

REFERENCES

Albert, H., & Obler, L. (1978). <u>The bilingual brain:
Neuropsychological and neurolinguistic aspects of bilingualism</u>.
New York: Academic Press.

Almanza, H., & Mosley, W. (1980). Curriculum adaptations and
modifications for culturally diverse handicapped children.
<u>Exceptional Children</u>. <u>46</u>, 608-614.

Ambert, A., & Dew, N. (1982). <u>Special education for exceptional
bilingual students: A handbook for educators</u>. Milwaukee: Midwest
National Origin Desegregation Assistance Center.

Asher, J. (1979). <u>Learning another language through actions: The
complete teacher's guidebook</u>. Los Gatos CA: Skyoak Productions.

Askins, B. (1978). <u>Responsive Environment Early Education Program
(REEEP). Third-year evaluation study: Final evaluation report,
1977-1978</u>. Santa Fe: New Mexico State Department of Education.

Baca, L. (1980). <u>Policy options for insuring the delivery of an
appropriate education to handicapped children who are of limited
English proficiency</u>. Reston VA: The Council for Exceptional
Children.

Baca, M. (1974). What's going on in the bilingual special education
classroom? <u>TEACHING Exceptional Children</u>, <u>7</u>, 25.

Benson, C. S., Medrich, E. A., & Buckley, S. (1980). A new view of school
efficiency: Household time contributions to school achievement. In
J. W. Guthrie (Ed.), <u>School finance policies and practices. The
1980s: A decade of conflict</u> (pp. 169-204). Cambridge MA:
Ballinger Publishing Company.

Bland, E., Sabatino, D., Sedlack, R., & Sterberg, L. (1979).
Availability, usability, and desirability of instructional materials
and media for minority handicapped students. <u>The Journal of
Special Education</u>, <u>13</u>, 157-167.

Brown, G., Rose, N., Hill, S., & Olivas, M. (1980). <u>The condition of
education for Hispanic Americans</u>. Washington, DC: National
Center for Education Statistics.

Bruck, M. (1978). The suitability of early French immersion programs for
the language disabled child. <u>The Canadian Modern Language
Review</u>, <u>34</u>, 884-887.

Bryen, D. (1974). Special education and the linguistically different
child. <u>Exceptional Children</u>, <u>40</u>, 589-599.

Bushman R., & Madsen, H. (1976). A description and evaluation of
Suggestopedia--A new teaching methodology. In J. Fanselow & R. Crymes
(Eds.), <u>On TESOL '76</u> (pp. 29-38). Washington DC: TESOL.

Chan, K., & Rueda, R. (1979). Poverty and culture in education: Separate but equal. _Exceptional Children_, _45_, 422-428.

Chance, P. (1981). The remedial thinker. _Psychology Today_. _16_, 63-73.

Chinn, P. (1979a). Curriculum development for culturally different exceptional children. _Teacher Education and Special Education_, _2_(4), 49-58.

Chinn, P. (1979b). The exceptional minority child: Issues and some answers. _Exceptional Children_, _45_, 532-536.

Cummins, J. (1981). Four misconceptions about language proficiency in bilingual education. _Journal of the National Association for Bilingual Education_, _5_(3), 31-45.

Cummins, J. (1982). The role of primary language development in promoting educational success for language minority students. In _Schooling and language minority students: A theoretical framework_. Los Angeles: Bilingual Education Evaluation, Dissemination, and Assessment Center.

Cummins, J. (1983). Bilingualism and special education: Program and pedagogical issues. _Learning Disabilities Quarterly_, _6_, 373-386.

Deignan, M., & Ryen, K. (1979). _Annotated bibliography of bilingual teaching materials applicable to the special learning needs of Spanish-dominant special education pupils_. Portsmouth NH: New England Teacher Corps Network.

DeLeon, J. (1983). _Evaluating and adapting materials for use with bilingual exceptional children_. Paper presented at the meeting of The Council for Exceptional Children, Detroit, Michigan.

Dew, N. (1981). _Specialized curriculum materials for exceptional bilingual children_. Arlington Heights IL: Illinois Resource Center for Exceptional Bilingual Children.

Dew N. (1983). _Components of a quality intervention program for LEP exceptional students_. Unpublished training material. (Available from Illinois Resource Center for Bilingual Exceptional Children, Arlington Heights, Illinois).

Diggs, R. (1974). Education across cultures. _Exceptional Children_, _40_, 578-583.

Dulay, H., Burt, M., & Krashen, S. (1982). _Language two_. New York: Oxford Unversity Press.

Feuerstein, R. (1980). _Instrumental enrichment: An intervention program for cognitive modifiability_. Baltimore: University Park Press.

Garcia, S. (1983). <u>Effects of student characteristics, school programs</u>
<u>and organization of decision making for placement of Hispanic</u>
<u>students in classes for the learning disabled.</u> Doctoral
dissertation, in preparation, The University of Texas at Austin.

Garcia, S. (1984). <u>Effects of student characteristics, school programs,</u>
<u>and organization on decisionmaking for the placement of Hispanic</u>
<u>students in classes for the learning disabled.</u> Unpublished doctoral
dissertation, The University of Texas at Austin, Austin.

Good, T., & Brophy, J. (1973). <u>Looking in classrooms.</u> New York:
Harper & Row.

Greenlee, M. (1981). Specifying the needs of a 'bilingual'
developmentally disabled population: Issues and case studies. <u>The</u>
<u>Journal of the National Association for Bilingual Education,</u> <u>6</u>(1),
55-76.

Hammill, D., & Bartel, N. (Eds.). (1971). <u>Educational perspectives in</u>
<u>learning disabilities.</u> New York: John Wiley & Sons.

Harth, R. (1982). The Feuerstein perspective on the modification of
cognitive performance. <u>Focus on Exceptional Children,</u> <u>15</u>,(3),
1-12.

Henderson, R. (1980). Social and emotional needs of culturally diverse
children. <u>Exceptional Children,</u> <u>46</u>, 598-605.

Jaramillo, M. (1974). Cultural conflict curriculum and the exceptional
child. <u>Exceptional Children,</u> <u>40</u>, 585-587.

Johnson, T., & Krug, K. (1980). Integrative and instrumental motivations
in search of a measure. In J. Oller & K. Perkins (Eds.), <u>Research</u>
<u>in language testing.</u> Rowley MA: Newbury House.

Krashen, S. (1982). Bilingual education and second language acquisition
theory. In <u>Schooling and language minority students: A</u>
<u>theoretical framework.</u> Los Angeles: Bilingual Education
Evaluation, Dissemination, and Assessment Center.

Krashen, S., & Terrell, T. (1983). <u>The natural approach: Language</u>
<u>acquisition in the classroom.</u> Oxford England: Pergamon Press.

Lerman, R., & Cortez, E. (1978). <u>Discovering and meeting the needs of</u>
<u>Hispanic hearing impaired children.</u> (ERIC Document Reproduction
Service No. ED 155-292)

Maldonado, E. (1984). <u>A comparison of assessment, placement, and</u>
<u>services provided Hispanics and non-Hispanics in speech, hearing, and</u>
<u>language programs.</u> Unpublished doctoral dissertation, University
of Massachusetts, Amherst.

McConnell, B. (1981). IBI (Individualized Bilingual Instruction): A validated program model effective with bilingual handicapped children. Paper presented at The Council for Exceptional Children Conference on the Exceptional Bilingual Child, New Orleans, LA.

Muller, M. (1975). Itinerant bilingual services program for Title I eligible CRMD children. Brooklyn: New York City Board of Education, Office of Educational Evaluation.

National Clearinghouse for Bilingual Education (NCBE). (1984, June 6). Second language teaching. Memo, p. 1-4.

Ortiz, A. (1981). Development and implementation of IEPs for exceptional bilingual children. In J. Nazzaro (Ed.), Culturally diverse exceptional children in school. Reston VA: The Council for Exceptional Children.

Ortiz, A. (1984). Choosing the language of instruction for exceptional bilingual children. TEACHING Exceptional Children, 16, 208-212.

Ortiz, A., & Yates, J. (1982). Teacher training associated with serving bilingual exceptional students. Teacher Education and Special Education, 5(3), 61-68.

Ortiz, A., & Yates, J. (1984). Staffing and the development of individualized education programs for bilingual exceptional students. In L. M. Baca & H. T. Cervantes (Eds.), The bilingual special education interface (pp. 187-212). St. Louis: Times Mirror/Mosby College Publishing.

Plata, M. (1979). Preparing teachers for the Mexican American handicapped: The challenge and the charge. Teacher Education and Special Education, 2(4), 21-26.

Rist, R. (1970). Student social class and teacher expectations: The self-fulfilling prophecy in ghetto education. Harvard Educational Review, 40, 411-450.

Rodriguez, R., Cole, J., Stile, S., & Gallegos, R. (1979). Bilingualism and biculturalism for the special education classroom. Teacher Education and Special Education, 2(4), 69-74.

Rotter, J. (1966). Generalized expectancies for internal versus external control of reinforcement. Psychological Monographs, 80(1), 1-28.

Rubenzer, R. (1979). The role of the right hemisphere in learning and creativity: Implications for enhancing problem solving ability. The Gifted Child Quarterly, 23(1), 78-100.

Sanua, U. (1976). <u>Bilingual programs for the physically handicapped,</u>
    <u>school year 1974-1975</u>. Brooklyn: New York City Board of
    Education.

Secada, W. (in press). The language of instruction for hearing impaired
    students from non-English speaking homes. In G. Delgado (Ed.), <u>The</u>
    <u>Hispanic deaf -- Issues and Challenges</u>. Washington DC:
    Gallaudet College Press.

Silvernail, D. (1979). <u>Teaching styles as related to student</u>
    <u>achievement</u>. Washington DC: National Education Association.

Tikunoff, W. (1982). <u>The significant bilingual instructional features</u>
    <u>descriptive study: Progress and issues from Part I</u>. Paper
    presented at the meeting of the American Educational Research
    Association, New York.

Vasquez, J. (1975). Locus of control, social class and learning. <u>In</u>
    <u>School desegregation and cultural pluralism: Perspectives on</u>
    <u>progress</u>. San Francisco: Service, Training, and Research in
    Desegregated Education, Far West Laboratory for Educational Research
    & Development.

Weiss, R. (1980). <u>Efficacy and cost effectiveness of an early</u>
    <u>intervention program for young handicapped children</u>. Paper
    presented at the meeting of the Handicapped Children's Early
    Education Program (HCEEP) Project Directors, Washington, D.C.

CHAPTER 5

TEACHER EDUCATION PROGRAMS

Leonard Baca

One of the greatest priorities for educators is the task of providing the most appropriate and effective educational programs and experience for various student populations. Up to the present time, one population of students that has been largely ignored has been the exceptional bilingual. In this paper, exceptional and handicapped are used interchangeably. "Exceptional" includes students who are handicapped in a variety of ways: the mentally retarded, the learning disabled, the emotionally disturbed, the physically handicapped, and the visually and hearing impaired. In addition to these handicapping conditions, however, bilingual exceptional students come from culturally and linguistically different backgrounds and have not acquired proficiency in the English language. This population may be best described as culturally and linguistically different exceptional students (CLDE). Although the actual number of CLDE students is not known, an estimate of this number was obtained during a 1976 national study concerning the overlap of identified Title I students and Title VII students. According to the results of the study, approximately one-half million students aged 5 to 21 years were handicapped and from non-English language backgrounds (National Center for Educational Statistics, 1980).

To teach these students in the language they can best understand is to build on their linguistic and cultural strengths and is compatible with sound educational practice. During the past 50 years, a great deal of emphasis has been placed on the education of handicapped students through various special education programs. This movement reached its peak in 1974, with the passage of P.L. 94-142, The Education for All Handicapped Children Act. The education of handicapped children continues to be a strong national priority. Even more recently, within the past 15 years, there has been a renewed interest in bilingual education. The United States Congress passed the Bilingual Education Act (P.L. 90-247) in 1968. This act made it possible for local school districts to receive federal funding for the implementation of bilingual programs designed to meet the needs of students with limited English proficiency.

Recent developments in litigation and educational research dealing with handicapped children of limited English proficiency suggests that educators must seriously address the issues related to designing and implementing bilingual special education programs. One of the most critical needs in this overall national effort is to prepare a cadre of high-quality, trained, bilingual special education teachers who will be able to provide the necessary educational experiences that will assist these students in developing to their fullest potential.

Any discussion of bilingual special education teacher training should occur within the broader context of multicultural education. In 1979, multicultural teacher training was formally institutionalized by the National Council for Accreditation of Teacher Education (NCATE). This influential accreditation agency adopted a multicultural education policy statement which requires all teacher training programs to include a multicultural component. Since this requirement is relatively new, many schools of education are still in the beginning stages of planning and implementing the component. With time and careful implementation this requirement will have a significant impact on teacher preparation programs. At the heart of multicultural education is the concept of cultural pluralism. Advocates of this concept endorse the principle that there is no model American. Cultural pluralism not only appreciates but promotes cultural diversity. It recognizes the unique contributions of various cultural groups that have strengthened and enriched our society.

Ten years ago the Commission on Multicultural Education of the American Association of Colleges for Teacher Education also adopted an important policy statement. One of the paragraphs of this statement is particularly significant. It reads as follows:

> To endorse cultural pluralism is to endorse the principle that there is no one model American. To endorse cultural pluralism is to understand and appreciate the differences that exist among the nation's citizens. It is to see these differences as a positive force in the continuing development of a society which professes a wholesome respect for the intrinsic worth of every individual. Cultural pluralism is more than a temporary accommodation to placate racial and ethnic minorities. It is a concept that aims toward a heightened sense of being and wholeness of the entire society based on the unique strength of each of its parts. (AACTE, 1973, p. 264)

Bilingual special education teacher training is one strategy for promoting cultural pluralism in our schools. More importantly, it is an effort designed to promote equal educational opportunity for limited-English-proficient students who are also handicapped.

As an emerging discipline, bilingual special education draws heavily from both bilingual education and special education. Both of these fields have been very actively involved in teacher training activities for many years. Bilingual special education teacher training, however, requires much more than the borrowing of courses from each of the parent disciplines. Bilingual special education requires a carefully articulated and planned convergence of these two disciplines which results in a new and unique body of knowledge.

RECENT HISTORY OF BILINGUAL SPECIAL EDUCATION TEACHER TRAINING

The problem of preparing high-quality teachers, teacher trainers, and other leadership personnel in this specialized area is not new and has already been addressed by the Office of Special Education as well as by a few universities and colleges throughout the country.

In 1978, the Bureau for the Handicapped of the Department of Education, cognizant of the scarcity of qualified bilingual/bicultural personnel, took steps to correct the situation. Through its Hispanic initiative, which was later extended to other linguistically and culturally different groups as well, the bureau encouraged the establishment of personnel preparation programs which would both recruit and train bilingual/bilcultural professionals to work with CLDE students. In 1979, an initial group of 22 personnel preparation programs were funded under this initiative. Since then, the number has increased annually. Thus, while there were a few programs functioning prior to the initiative, in a real sense the preparation of personnel to work with CLDE began in 1979. As in any new field, there is a need to identify, define, and improve current practices.

In the spring of 1980 and again in the spring of 1981, professionals engaged in preparing personnel to work with CLDE students met in the Washington, D.C. area in workshops sponsored by ACCESS, INC., and funded by the Department of Education. Some of the purposes of the two workshops were to define the field, determine the competencies which should be required of both trainers and trainees, and share ideas about philosophies and methodology. According to Grossman (1982), one of the results of these workshops was an agreement to replace the term bilingual special education with the term "the education of culturally and linguistically different exceptional students," a phrase which emphasizes cultural as well as linguistic differences. It was also agreed that persons preparing to work with such students need to have the skills included in the field of bilingual/bicultural education, special education, and a third group of cross-cultural "convergent" skills which were not found in either but are vital to working with CLDES.

Three examples of the need for the third component follow. In the area of assessment, bilingual/bicultural educators may receive training in the assessment of language dominance and proficiency. They may also be prepared to assess and develop academic readiness and achievement in both their students' first and second languages. As one aspect of their training, special educators are prepared to assess academic proficiency in language arts and assess and remediate learning disabilities involving language development using instruments and procedures developed for

English-speaking acculturated monocultural students. However, neither the bilingual/bicultural educator nor the special educator is trained in the assessment and development of language when this development is impaired in some manner and the child is not from an English-speaking home. Persons who complete both a bilingual/bilcultural training program still will not be equipped to use culturally and linguistically appropriate special education assessment and instructional procedures with non-English-speaking CLDES.

In the area of counseling, counselors who work with students are trained to determine when their counselee's problems are intrinsically or extrinsically caused. When the cause of the students' problems are intrinsic (within the students) they may try to help the students accept the responsibility, blame, and guilt for their actions, and/or help them believe that they can control their own lives. When the causes are extrinsic (outside the students) they may encourage the students to assert themselves, to use methods to change their environments, or not to assume responsibility and guilt for things which may be beyond their control. When CLDES react to prejudicial treatment and cultural conflicts by withdrawing or rebelling, counselors who are unaware of the prejudices and cultural conflicts which these students face may assume that the cause of their behavior is intrinsic. As a result, they may use techniques design to change the students' shy or agressive personalities instead of using techniques to help them deal more effectively with a hostile or insensitive environment.

As a final example, teachers or counselors who are unaware that in some cultures it is a sign of disrespect to express a lack of understanding or a difference of opinion may believe that students or parents who politely act as if they understand and agree actually do understand and accept the suggestions made to them. In fact, they may neither agree nor understand. This type of cross-cultural misunderstanding can have serious consequences in assessment, instruction, and parent involvement.

Having identified these three groups of competencies, those included in bilingual/bilcultural education, those included in special education, and those convergent/cross-cultural abilities not included in either of the two traditional fields, the participants in the ACCESS workshops enumerated specific competencies within each of these three components which should characterize both trainers and well prepared trainees. When the trainers evaluated themselves, it was clear that, with very few exceptions, they had not acquired all of these competencies. Typically, trainers had been trained in either bilingual/bicultural education or special education, but not in both, and not in convergent skills. Those few who were trained in both areas tended to lack some of the cross-cultural competencies not included in either area; each trainer had his or her strengths and weaknesses. It becomes clear that a number of models of personnel preparation were being used.

It is also interesting to note that there was a significant difference between the mean responses of the bilingual directors as compared to the special education directors on 15 of the 27 competency items. In general, the bilingual directors rated the importance of using the native language and culture as well as ESL methodology and parental involvement significantly higher than the special education directors.

A careful review of several competency-related studies indicates that there are certain competencies that are repeatedly ranked as very important by multiple sources. In other words, there seems to be consensus in the literature that the following are the most important general competencies for bilingual special educators.

1. The desire to work with the CLDE student.

2. The ability to work effectively with parents of CLDE students.

3. The ability to develop appropriate IEP's for the CLDE student.

4. Knowledge and sensitivity toward the language and the culture of the group to be served.

5. The ability to teach ESL to CLDE students.

6. The ability to conduct nonbiased assessment with CLDE students.

7. The ability to use appropriate methods and materials when working with CLDE students.

The most detailed and specific set of competencies that have been developed are compatible with the most frequently cited generic competencies listed above. These very specific competencies were prepared by an expert panel of bilingual special education teacher trainers convened by the Association for Cross-Cultural Education and Social Studies (ACCESS) (Pynn, 1981). These competencies are as follows:

I. Instruction/Curriculum

    A. The trainee is knowledgeable about general cultural characteristics:

        1. Lifestyles of ethnic minority populations, family structure, and community support systems.

        2. Attitudes and behaviors of cultural and socioeconomic groups.

    B. The trainee understands the relevance of child-rearing practices of ethnic minority families to the CLDE child's cognitive, emotional, and social development.

    C. The trainee is aware of cultural conflicts resulting from ethnic minority differences that may affect the CLDE child's self-image and thus influence his or her emotional and social development.

D. The trainee institutes a teaching process that takes into account the impact of cultural conflicts on the CLDE child's academic performance.

E. The trainee understands the acculturation process of culturally diverse individuals into the mainstream of American society.

F. The trainee implements techniques to facilitate the integration of the CLDE child into American schools and society.

G. The trainee develops and implements appropriate educational programs to meet the special needs of the CLDE children.

H. The trainee develops educational programs, designed to improve the bilingual development of learning disabled children, which reflect an understanding of current approaches in the field.

I. The trainee plans, designs, and implements special education programs for CLDE populations in accordance with legislative requirements and guidelines.

J. The trainee will plan, design, and implement individualized education programs which include, where appropriate, such subject areas as: language arts, arithmetic, science, social studies, vocational skills, and physical education.

K. The trainee develops and applies appropriate educational methods based, in part, upon diagnostic results.

L. The trainee demonstrates skill in developing and/or adapting educational materials and procedures to meet individual needs.

M. The trainee works in cooperation with other education professionals to design a full-service educational program appropriate to the needs of students exhibiting specific handicaps, gifts, or talents.

N. The trainee designs curriculum and instructional programs that are based on behavioral objectives considering cultural variables.

O. The trainee directs and organizes program activities in cooperation with parents, teachers, and other school personnel.

P. The trainee determines the appropriate instructional setting to maximize the educational development of the CLDE child.

II. Assessment and Evaluation

A. The trainee recognizes normal language development patterns.

B. The trainee is knowledgeable about major empirical research in the area of speech and language acquisition.

C. The trainee explains the effects of anatomic, physiologic, linguistic, psycholinguistic, and sociolinguistic factors on the communication process.

D. The trainee differentiates between those difficulties arising from second language acquisition and those from speech and language disability.

   1. Trainee distinguishes between culturally derived linguistic conventions and deviant language development problems.

   2. Trainee understands the nature, etiologies, and remedial techniques associated with language disorders.

E. The trainee writes descriptive reports which accurately reflect the nature of communicative disorders.

F. The trainee demonstrates the ability to assess student strengths and needs within the cognitive, affective, and psychomotor domains through the use of appropriate formal and informal instruments and procedures (e.g., standardized tests, commercially prepared informal tests, teacher-prepared measures, and criterion-referenced measures).

G. The trainee is aware of the uses and limitations of current standard assessment techniques in regard to CLDE populations.

H. The trainee develops an assessment model based on information gained from several sources. For example:

   1. Anecdotal records and pupil behavior scales.

   2. Observations and recommendations from parents, teachers, and other school personnel.

I. The trainee is able to assess those factors limiting the participation of the family in the school setting and set specific goals.

J. The trainee formulates an accurate description of student ability based upon observation of academic performance in light of the CLDE student's cultural background.

K. The trainee is aware of the influence of learning styles, cultural values, and language patterns of ethnic and minority groups on classroom and test performance.

L. The trainee administers appropriate language assessment instruments and accurately interprets the skills measured and the information obtained.

M. The trainee uses the information gained to determine the CLDE student's most appropriate and least restrictive educational setting.

N. The trainee uses a cognitive style analysis approach as a diagnostic-prescriptive tool.

O. The trainee will write a diagnostic evaluation in behavioral terms.

P. The trainee will analyze skills and educational materials through the task analysis approach to determine program effectiveness.

Q. The trainee develops and applies appropriate educational methods based, in part, upon diagnostic results.

R. The trainee determines the appropriate instructional strategies used in diagnostic-prescriptive teaching of the CLDE child.

S. The trainee develops techniques to improve communication competence within the classroom.

1. Trainee understands the function of language in the classroom as it relates to educational development.

2. Trainee develops alternative techniques to improve specific speech and language skills of CLDE children.

T. The trainee implements the appropriate strategies for the diagnostic-prescriptive teaching of CLDE children.

U. The trainee reviews the effectiveness of instructional methods implemented within the special education program for CLDE children.

V. The trainee evaluates, using appropriate measurement devices, the effectiveness of diagnostic programs for CLDE individuals.

1. Trainee examines materials, academic tasks, and methodologies using a task analysis approach.

2. Trainee examines the contributions of other resources (e.g., parents, teachers, and other school personnel).

W. The trainee evalutes the impact of prescribed treatments by
    means of an initial and continuing analysis of changes in
    academic and personal growth: e.g., trainee utilizes such
    data-collecting devices as questionnaires, rating scales, and
    checklists.

X. The trainee modifies objectives and learning approaches,
    provided such changes are indicated by the ongoing evaluation
    of educational plans.

III. Classroom Management

A. The trainee is aware of how nonverbal behaviors of both CLDE
    children and nonethnic teachers may lead to miscommunication
    between children and teachers.

B. The trainee understands and applies interaction and management
    strategies (e.g., behavior modification, group dynamics,
    interaction analysis behavior therapy, and life space
    management therapy) in light of cultural, socioeconomic, and
    language factors influencing behavior.

C. The trainee develops and applies appropriate educational
    methods based, in part, upon diagnostic results.

D. The trainee demonstrates a thorough knowledge of critical
    issues relative to effective classroom management. The
    following issues are suggested:

    1. Effective teaching methodologies.

    2. Modeling of appropriate/desirable behaviors.

    3. Self-realization and values clarification.

    4. Understanding of and sensitivity to physical, social,
        developmental, and cultural factors.

    5. Emotional climate in the learning environment.

    6. Teacher flexibility as demonstrated through the use of
        alternative activity suggestions, willingness to give
        explanations and reasons, and the encouragement of student
        input.

E. The trainee examines behavior management models or approaches
    and selects those appropriate to individual needs.

F. The trainee implements educational management strategies, such
    as: learning centers, material coding, student self-directed
    activities, and continuous-progress management.

G. The trainee examines educational management systems with respect to:

   1. Own cultural perspective.

   2. Perspective of the CLDE child.

   3. Potential biases (e.g., ethnic, class, cultural, and/or linguistic).

   4. Potential discriminatory effects of using a specific behavior and classroom management model.

H. The trainee extends the behavioral management program through collaborative efforts with the home, community agencies, and state and federal agencies.

IV. Counseling

A. The trainee assists parents in identifying their CLDE child's learning difficulties.

B. The trainee, with the support of parents and teachers, develops goals and objectives and prescribes special programs to meet individual needs.

C. The trainee provides parents with information on available community resources.

D. The trainee extends the behavioral management program through collaborative efforts with the home, community agencies, and state and federal agencies.

E. The trainee gathers pertinent information and provides training to the CLDE child's family, teachers, other professionals, and national, state, and local groups: e.g., trainee develops a system for ongoing technical and professional support to ancillary educational personnel.

F. The trainee assists families and their CLDE children in understanding and dealing with the attitudes, lifestyles, behaviors, and educational philosophy of American society and its schools.

V. Advocacy/Public Relations

A. The trainee understands the historical development of and legal basis for bilingual and special edcuation. The trainee, for example, has knowledge and understanding of the following:

1. Public Law 94-142.

2. Rehabilitation Act of 1973, Section 504.

3. Title VII legislation.

4. _Lau v. Nichols_ case and other pertinent legislation.

B. The trainee explains significant implications of special education regulations to students, parents, educators, and others.

C. The trainee explains the legal implications of significant court decisions on policy development and legislative reform to students, parents, educators, and others.

D. The trainee gathers pertinent information and provides training to the CLDE child's family, teachers, other professionals, and national, state, and local groups: e.g., trainee develops a system for ongoing technical and professional support to ancillary educational personnel.

E. The trainee makes suggestions to school personnel and local education agencies for implementing appropriate instructional programs which are sensitive to the needs of the CLDE child.

F. The trainee provides parents with information on available community resources.

VI. Research

A. The trainee understands all aspects of teaching CLDE children, including the recent research, etiology, content areas, educational procedure, and support systems necessary for effective educational management.

B. The trainee demonstrates knowledge of significant theory and research applications relative to teaching CLDE children by developing and implementing clinical/prescriptive activities.

CHARACTERISTICS OF CURRENT TRAINING PROGRAMS

A study conducted by the Multicultural Special Education Project (MUSEP) in 1982 collected data from 30 bilingual and/or multicultural special education teacher training projects at the university level. These projects were all located in the Western region of the United States and were funded through the Division of Personnel Preparation, Office of Special Education, U.S. Department of Education. The return rate (seven projects) was 23% (about average) and adequately represented the broad range of projects. This data provides a representative profile of bilingual special education projects in the Western region. Based on the responses to the questionnaire, each project was identified as belonging in one of three general categories:

1. A strictly traditional special education program with recruitment of ethnic or bilingual students; for example, a program that trains regular learning disability teachers but attempts to recruit minority and bilingual students.

2. A traditional special education program with bilingual special education curriculum infused into existing coursework and program requirements. This type of program, for example, would add a few lectures or modules and bibliographies on bilingual special education to existing courses.

3. A bilingual special education program that is specifically designed to train bilingual special education teachers and includes bilingual special education course work and field experiences with bilingual special education curriculum.

Analysis of the data indicates that 29% were strictly traditional special education programs that recruited minority students at most; 29% were traditional special education programs with bilingual special education infused into existing curricula; and 42% were bilingual special education programs that offered specific courses in bilingual special education and considered their program a bilingual special education program.

Table 1 summarizes the information on program types and shows the number of graduates for each of the programs.

TABLE 1
Program Types and Their Respective Graduates

Projects	Strictly Traditional Special Ed. Program With Recruitment of Ethnic Students	Traditional Special Ed. With Bilingual Special Ed. Infused Info. Existing Courses	Bilingual Special Education Program	Number of Students Graduated		
				B.A.	M.A.	Ph.D.
1			X	5	–	–
2		X		5	1	–
3		X		2	–	2
4	X			15	1	55
5	X			20	5	25
6			X	6	–	–
7			X	–	–	–
Total %	29%	29%	42%			

Traditional special education programs graduated the most students in each of the three training levels (BA - 35, MA - 6, PhD - 84), followed by infused traditional special education programs (BA - 7, MA - 1, PhD - 2). The low number of graduates from bilingual special education programs (BA - 11) indicates the relatively recent emergence of the field. More importantly, it points to the need for continued support of this specialized field. In terms of the degree of interdisciplinary emphasis in the curriculum, 86% of the students in all projects sampled were exposed to some ethnic language component (e.g., Spanish, Navajo, etc.); 71% were exposed to cultural sensitivity or awareness coursework (e.g., Asian or Chicano Studies); 57% were exposed to specific bilingual special education methodology; and 43% had interdisciplinary exchange with bilingual education.

It was stated that there is a general trend toward deemphasis of education by state and federal funding agencies. Without adequate resources it is very difficult to recruit students. It also appears that some faculty consider it necessary to deemphasize entrance standards and stress exit criteria in order to recruit and retain students. The problem is compounded because of the small pool of high school graduates from which to draw.

Public school support for bilingual special education programs is also a problem. Many indicated that public schools in some areas do not support bilingual special education efforts by higher education institutions. Nonetheless, the public schools lack trained professionals in bilingual special education. University training programs need to be strengthed in order to attract students and help relieve this shortage of personnel. There is also a critical need to infuse teacher training programs with a bilingual special education content. This also involves increasing faculty awareness and support. Clarifying the interface between bilingual education and special education is a high priority.

In the area of research basic knowledge is needed about target populations, e.g., American Indians, Hispanics, and Asians. Specifically, more information is needed about their culture, language, and cognitive development. It was agreed that more knowledge is needed concerning what constitutes a positive learning atmosphere for children being serviced through bilingual special education. Research is needed on effective teacher training models for bilingual special education.

In the area of program development, it was emphasized that there should be a coordinated effort on the part of bilingual special education training programs and school districts to communicate with state personnel, to make known the needs of bilingual special education in the schools. This should encourage institutionalization and help secure funding at both levels. In order to achieve meaningful local control, it was stressed that IHE's, school boards, school administrators, teachers, bilingual teachers, bilingual special education teachers, parents, and the general public all need to be sensitized to the issue and need for bilingual special education programs that reflect local needs.

Bilingual special education teacher trainers need to be knowledgeable about bilingual/bicultural and special education, in addition to being versed in bilingual special education per se. For example, teacher trainers should be "equipped" to use culturally and linguistically appropriate special education assessment procedures with non-English-speaking culturally and linguistically different exceptional students (CLDES). It is extremely important that bilingual special education trainers and programs maintain and increase communication among themselves. Communication will enhance camaraderie, program support, avoid duplication of mistakes and efforts in research, and will keep morale up in these times of scarce resources.

The existing heterogeneity among bilingual special education projects is an asset that can aid us in our search for successful project components. Recognized is the fact that these evaluations will not turn up an ideal project that will be suited for all regions and ethnic groups.

Finally, it was stressed that there is a need to begin to make specific efforts to institutionalize projects that are dependent on grants, i.e., soft monies. In order to do this, four things should be emphasized: cause awareness, acceptance, participation, and demonstration of the effectiveness and need of bilingual special education projects.

Additional data on these teacher training projects was acquired through site visits to the projects as well as through personal communication. Table 2 summarizes the major concerns and the recurring needs expressed by the project directors.

As can be seen in Table 2, the most common concern among all projects was the institutionalization of their training programs. Fifty-nine percent of the projects expressed some concern that they would cease to exist unless adopted by their institutions and departments and made permanent programs.

A second most recurrent concern among the 17 projects was student recruitment and support. Forty-nine percent of the projects felt there were not enough minority students in their programs and had problems recruiting them. Moreover, some projects felt a need to provide academic and general support to the few minorities that were already in the programs.

Table 2 indicates that 35% of the projects felt they needed the support and cooperation of academic and nonacademic departments, programs, and agencies, such as special education departments, state departments, LEA's, school districts, and community groups. Twenty-four percent felt bilingual special education programs needed better planning and development. Another 24% of the projects felt a need to infuse bilingual special education curricula into existing course of existing and institutionalized training programs, such as special and bilingual education programs.

114

Table 2
Needs and Concerns Generated From Site Visits

Percentage	Expressed Need
59%*	Program institutionalization.
49%	Student recruitment and support (e.g., tutoring).
35%	Program support and cooperation with departments, programs, and agencies (e.g., state departments, LEA's, school districts, and communities).
24%	Program planning and development.
24%	Infusion of bilingual special education curricula into existing courses.
18%	Faculty and teacher inservice training: models and content.
18%	Research and development of reliable and valid diagnostic instruments in bilingual special education.
18%	Method and curricula identification, dissemination, and development appropriate for bilingual special education.
12%	Basic research emphasis.

*Many institutions had more than one concern.

Eighteen percent felt that models and content of inservice training for faculty and teachers are important and in need of development. Yet another 18% felt there is a need in bilingual special education to research and develop reliable and valid diagnostic instruments that are sensitive to culturally and linguistically different populations. Still another 18% of the projects felt a need to identify, disseminate, and develop teaching methods and curricula appropriate for teachers to use in the area of bilingual special education. Finally, 12% of the projects felt that the area of bilingual special education needs to be involved and should serve as a catalyst for basic empirical research.

PROGRAM PLANNING AND INSTITUTIONALIZATION

To "institutionalize" a newly establish or nontraditional program like bilingual special education in higher education means to make it a regular part of the program offerings of a college or university. The institutionalization process is never automatic; to accomplish it, a strategy or plan of action, frequently extending over several years, is required. If a strategy is to have reasonable probability of success, careful attention must be given to meeting five conditions. If these conditions are not met, the probability of a successful plan is substantially reduced. These conditions are described below from the viewpoint of the person interested in institutionalizing a program.

Develop Central Office Administrative Support

Central offices serve as communication centers and as the locus of control of dollar and personnel resources. These resources tend to flow along the line of communication. For this reason, the director of a nontraditional program needs to have numerous interactions with the head of his or her unit. These meetings should be open to any topic related to the new program, including personnel matters, political issues, student support, long-term directions, publications, needed contracts, whether or not to pursue grant opportunities, presentations at national meetings, and the financial condition of the department and school. Such interactions have two important outcomes. First, each person leaves the meeting with a good sense of what is happening in the other person's domain. Second, incipient problems are dealt with before they occur, thus leading to better management.

Pay Attention to Political Circumstances

Many programs, especially those involving bilingualism and ethnic groups, are very sensitive to shifts in viewpoint or power within the university, the state, or the nation. For this reason, keeping one's political support in repair is an important aspect of institutionalizing a program. Three types of support are significant here: (a) grass roots, including parents, teachers, and school administrators; (b) power block, including subgroups of legislators or congressional representatives, and th support of state or federal agencies; and (c) support from other disciplines. These three groups must be kept well informed. In a university, the good will of other departments is critically important to survival and success. In the bilingual/multicultural special education area, forming solid relationships with foreign language departments, linguistics, sociolinguistics, anthropology, and speech science permits them to know what the program is doing and what the major concerns and goals are, and prevents feelings of suspicion and interdepartmental hostility frequently found in colleges and universities when nontraditional programs arise.

The art of politics is finding a common value among groups such as those mentioned above. It is not always easy to do so since each political group is likely to form a set of values different from the other. That, one supposes, is what a "political group" means. To find a common value means that one must spend sufficient time with each type of group to be able to form several ideas about where the common ground among them might lie, should political action be required. While time consuming, the task of finding a common value is frequently a critical one for the director and staff of a nontraditional program like bilingual special education.

Find or Develop a Niche for the Program and Its Faculty

To feel secure in an organization, most persons need to have a home base or a special niche in the organization from which they can carry on their activities. The same seems to be true of programs. To develop a niche for a nontraditional program and its faculty is one of the most difficult tasks in institutionalization. To gain a niche, several important events need to occur between the central office, the appropriate academic unit, and the program. The first is the establishment of an academically sound and supportive academic base in an appropriate academic department or division. Not only must there be a good academic fit between the program and the department, but there should be a faculty support for the program from colleagues within the department. The second is identifying a carefully located space which is the visible office of the program, as space is the symbol of institutionalization. Third is developing program uniqueness. These issues are raised by a traditional program currently facing phase-out. One of its major problems is that the content of the program has, over the years, begun to appear in other programs, thus gradually reducing the uniqueness of the original program. People have asked, "What does this program do that is not done in other programs?" If this question is difficult to answer, either a program has never gained a niche or it is in danger of losing the one formerly occupied.

Consolidate Resources and Monitor Their Status Often

All college and university programs need three types of resources: faculty, students, and money. To consolidate faculty resources means that the faculty members involved in the program identify with it and are reliable in the sense that they will expend effort to improve the program rather than directing their attention elsewhere. To consolidate faculty resources requires the systematic application of leadership skills by the program director so that the faculty involved believe that their work is important, that it will be rewarded, and that the program has direction and social value.

The consolidation of student resources represents one of the most difficult problems of nontraditional programs. A key factor in the durability of federally sponsored programs for Hispanic and Native American peoples, for example, is that many of the funds are directly devoted to student support. Economically disadvantaged persons in these groups often cannot easily opt for higher education since doing so involves foregoing the money that would be gained from full-time employment while at the same time having to pay for more schooling. A subsidy, typically from federal sources, is therefore required if programs for these people are to have students. A withdrawal of this subsidy predicts program failure by dint of insufficient students from the target populations. Maintenance of direct federal or state subsidies for students is, therefore, a central reason for the development and maintenance of majority-minority political ties by minority group members. The major alternative to direct subsidies is the adaptation of nontraditional programs to the circumstances of its target population of students. This adaptation usually means a part-time program in which students can enroll during the evening and may include the use of teleconference instruction in which courses or workshops are delivered to remote areas at time convenient for students.

The consolidation of financial resources usually requires two moves. First, be certain a significant portion of the program faculty are on "hard" rather than "soft" money. Faculty on hard money is usually taken as a significant sign of successful institutionalization. Second, regular ways of raising money by grants, gifts, consulting, or contracts should be planned by the program faculty. Such funds frequently make the difference between a quality program and one chronically on the brink of financial disaster.

Build a Sound Program

The first step in building a sound program is to avoid slipshod admission practices. A program is known by the quality of its graduates. If one admits slow students on the one hand or purely opportunistic ones on the other, it will become suspect both inside and outside the college or university. Placement will become difficult. The second step is to build a rational curriculum. Such a curriculum has two important features: a) It can be described and explained in the sense that the faculty can show how the curriculum is related to the goals and objectives of the program, and b) the curriculum actually produces a reasonable level of the skills, knowledges, and intellectual strategies which the program claims that it produces. The third step is to bridge the special program to the regular faculty and curriculum by formal as well as informal mechanisms. The curriculum should not be too highly specialized and should have anchors in both special and bilingual education. The fourth step is to hold an experimental and evaluative posture toward the curriculum. Every program can be designed to be better than it is. An experimental posture means that one forms hypotheses about changes that will improve the program, and carries them out. An evaluative posture means that the effects of these changes are carefully appraised to make certain they actually produce improvements in the program. A systems approach to program evaluation is recommended.

As the five conditions described above suggest, institutionalizing a program is neither an easy nor a certain process. Creating a strategy or action plan substantially increases the probability of success, while not doing so leaves one's chances to luck.

MODEL TRAINING PROGRAMS

There are two general approaches that can be used in addressing the need to prepare bilingual special education teachers. Existing teacher training faculty and programs in special education and bilingual education can consolidate their resources and service their programs to focus on the unique needs of exceptional bilingual students. This is currently being done by several universities throughout the country, as mentioned earlier in this paper. Another approach is to focus attention on the training of the trainers themselves. At the preservice doctoral level, a few universities are working with doctoral students on an ad hoc basis. These programs use existing doctoral training programs in special education and add an emphasis in bilingual special education through independent studies, specialized seminars, internships, and related research projects. Among the universities involved in this type of leadership training are The University of Arizona, Arizona State University, San Diego State University, The University of Colorado, The University of New Mexico, New Mexico State University, The University of Massachusetts, Boston University, New York University, and New York State University.

The Multicultural Institute for Change

In addition to such preservice training for faculty, Landurand (1982) has developed a very successful inservice training model for college and university faculty in the area of bilingual special education. Through a U. S. Department of Education special education dean's grant, Landurand established the Multicultural Institute for Change at Regis College in Weston, Massachusetts. The Institute's primary goal is to improve the quality of service to linguistically and culturally different children. Currently, the Institute is training 16 faculty members from six nearby colleges and universities in the theory and practical application of bilingual special education. The following program description is taken from a publication of the Multicultural Institute for Change (Landurand, 1982).

The instructional program of the Institute for Change consists of five major components: theoretical modular training, a local educational agency, practicum experience, a college practicum experience, and an integrative seminar. For each of the three years, the faculty trainees complete three modules: the correlated local school or agency practice, the college practicum, and the integrative seminar. Prior to initiating any of the components, each faculty trainee, with the assistance of the project staff, undergoes a diagnostic prescriptive assessment. Each trainee analyzes his or her particular areas of expertise, background in bilingual/bicultural issues, and favored learning style. In addition, for each of the tasks specified in the college component, the trainee evaluates what he or she has done in that area and develops objectives from a multicultural perspective for self-improvement for achieving that goal. Once these assessments are completed, each trainee, with the help of the Project Director and part-time staff, develops an individual training plan (ITP) to accomplish each of the components developed in the Institute for Change. Techniques such as individual and school case studies; role playing; group problem solving; and on-site local school, agency, and college practicum are utilized in training.

At the end of the 3-year project, the Regis College Institute for Change will provide insights as to the strategies necessary for successful training of faculty members in the content of bilingual/ bicultural special education. To date, the Institute staff can suggest the following to other institutions that might consider such training:

1. Involve the administrative staff from the beginning of the project. Without the support of the deans, the Institute for Change would not be able to expect high levels of commitment from faculty.

2. Offer training sessions that do not conflict with faculty members' busy schedules. In most cases, "retreats" provide faculty with the opportunity to concentrate on the issues and skills relative to bilingual/bicultural special education.

3. Provide experiences in the public schools and community in order to update faculty's perceptions of the needs of linguistic minorities in the local educational agencies.

4. Be prepared to deal with attitudes faculty members may bring to the training that reflect their perceptions of individuals from culturally different backgrounds. Staff members and consultants should have skills in group processes, especially as these skills relate to racism and biases that faculty may consciously or unconsciously possess.

5. Provide ongoing follow-up with faculty and administrative staff. Because faculty have many responsibilities, their completion of ITP's may be difficult without the constant support of the project's staff and consultants.

Because of the immediate need to train bilingual special education teachers the above mentioned model is highly recommended both as a short-term strategy and as a strategy for colleges and universities who wish to retrain existing faculty.

Bilingual Language Learning System (BLLS)

Another significant and model inservice training program has been undertaken by the American Speech, Language, and Hearing Association (ASHA). This project is also funded by the Office of Special Education of the U. S. Department of Education. The project is known as the Bilingual Language Learning System (BLLS). The description of the program which follows was adapted from the project summary disseminated by ASHA.

The Bilingual Language Learning System (BLLS) project has been designed as a national coordinated effort to meet this need and to improve the availability and quality of speech-language pathology and audiology services rendered to bilingual/bicultural Spanish-English children. Funded August 1, 1981, by Special Education Programs, United States Department of Education, the BLLS project is intended to provide a series of 2-day inservice training institutes and a training manual which discuss characteristics of Spanish and English language acquisition; how speech-language pathologists and audiologists may provide appropriate evaluation of Spanish-English children with suspected communication handicaps; how effective management strategies can be implemented for those children with confirmed language disorders; and how interaction of speech-language pathologists and audiologists with other school professionals can be promoted in order to increase the effectiveness of educational programming for this population.

During the course of the project, a model of training will be employed in which bilingual/bicultural speech-language pathologists will be trained to train other professionals. In addition, representatives of university/college training programs in speech-language pathology and audiology will be trained so that content of BLLS Institutes can be incorporated into university/college program curricula. State schools consultants will also be trained so that these resource persons can disseminate information on the BLSS Institutes and effect improved education for Spanish-English children. The Trainers, university/college representatives and school consultants, have been selected for the eight states which, collectively, account for nearly 90% of the Spanish-language population in the United States (Arizona, California, Colorado, Florida, Illinois, New Mexico, New York, and Texas). These individuals compose BLLS State Resource Teams in the eight target states.

During the first year of the project (August 1981 through May 1982), the BLLS training manual was developed and the State Resource Team members were selected. During the second year of the project (June 1982 through May 1983), the Trainers conducted a series of 14 BLLS Institutes for Hispanic bilingual and bilcultural speech-language pathologists, audiologists, and other Hispanic professionals who worked in teams with speech-language pathologists and audiologists, and selected a second group of Trainers for the project. During the third year of the project (June 1983 through May 1984), this second group were trained as Trainers and conducted a series of 22 BLLS Institutes for monolingual professionals. Training for bilingual/bicultural speech-language pathologists and audiologists will be distinct from training for monolingual individuals because the professional needs of the two groups are different.

The Institutes will serve to:

o   Disseminate state-of-the-art information regarding bilingual communication assessment and treatment to professionals working with Spanish-English children.

o   Provide opportunities for Trainers to develop their skills in presenting the curriculum content.

o   Field-test the original curriculum content so that necessary revision, based on evaluation by Institute participants, can be made.

As a result of BLLS training, it is anticipated that more speech-language pathologists and audiologists will provide improved services to bilingual/bicultural communicatively handicapped children. Greater consultative services will then be available to special and regular educators, and these professionals will better understand contributions that communication disorders specialists can provide.

RECOMMENDATIONS

1. Preservice training projects in bilingual special education should be given increased support from the local, state, and federal level.

2. Colleges and universities should cooperate with local school districts in conducting a planned and systematic inservice program in bilingual special education.

3. Leadership training in bilingual special education at the doctoral level should receive increased support from the U. S. Department of Education.

4. All types and levels of bilingual special education training should include a strong emphasis on parental involvement and parent training.

5. Bilingual special education teacher training curricula should be highly interdisciplinary in orientation, drawing not only from special education and bilingual education but from psychology, anthropology, linguistics, psycholinguistics, language departments, etc.

6. Bilingual special education teacher competencies identified as critical by practitioners should be validated empirically before being used to design future training programs.

7. Bilingual special education teacher training research should be conducted with particular emphasis given to student outcomes as the ultimate measure of success.

8. Teacher training materials and textbooks as well as bibliographies should be developed for the field of bilingual special education.

9. Training programs should make special provisions for student recruitment and retention. Stipends, tuition and book allowances, and additional support systems should also be provided.

10. Bilingual special education and ESL methods courses should be unique and different for this population of exceptional bilingual students.

11. The issue of dual (special education and bilingual education) endorsement and certification as well as bilingual special education endorsement and certification needs further study.

12. The training of regular education teachers through infusion regarding the needs of the bilingual exceptional child is a priority.

REFERENCES

American Association of Colleges in Teacher Education (AACTE). (1973). No one model American, Journal of Teacher Education, 24, 264.

Grossman, H. (1982). Bilingual special education teacher training. Summary of the Proceedings of the Bilingual Special Education Institute. Boulder CO: BUENO Center for Multicultural Education.

Landurand, P. (1982). Training Faculty in Bilingual Special Education, Regis College Multicultural Institute for Change.

MUSEP. (1982). A Report on Bilingual Special Education Teacher Training Programs, BUENO Center for Multicultural Education.

National Center for Educational Statistics (NCES). (1980). The condition of education. Washington DC: U.S. Government Printing Office.

Pynn, E. (1981). Bilingual Special Education Personnel Preparation National Teacher Oriented Seminar, ACCESS Inc.